STRATEGIC THINKING IN 3D

RELATED TITLES FROM POTOMAC BOOKS

Fighting Talk: Forty Maxims on War, Peace, and Strategy
—Colin S. Gray

National Security Dilemmas: Challenges and Opportunities
—Colin S. Gray

Military Strategy: Principles, Practices, and Historical Perspectives
—John M. Collins

STRATEGIC THINKING IN 3D

A Guide for National Security, Foreign Policy, and Business Professionals

ROSS HARRISON

Potomac Books
Washington, D.C.

Library of Congress Cataloging-in-Publication Data
Harrison, Ross, 1953–
  Strategic thinking in 3D : a guide for national security, foreign policy,
and business professionals / Ross Harrison. — First edition.
    p. cm
  Includes bibliographical references and index.
  ISBN 978-1-59797-706-7 (hbk. : alk. paper)
  ISBN 978-1-59797-807-1 (electronic)
  1. Strategy—Case studies. 2. Strategic culture. 3. Strategic planning. 4. Success
in business. 5. Qaida (Organization) 6. International relations. I. Title.
  U162.H296 2013
  658.4'012—dc23
                                                                    2013001937

Printed in the United States of America on acid-free paper that meets the American
National Standards Institute Z39-48 Standard.

Potomac Books
22841 Quicksilver Drive
Dulles, Virginia 20166

First Edition

10 9 8 7 6 5 4 3 2 1

This book is dedicated to my late father, **Roland Harrison**,
who gave me the room to think strategically;

To my mentor and teacher, the late **Richard Cottam**,
who introduced me to the rigors and mysteries of strategy;

And to my loving wife, **Mahnaz M. Harrison**,
whose unflagging love and support helped give me
the courage to write this book.

CONTENTS

PREFACE

Why write a book on strategy when so many have already been written? One motive for writing this book came from the reactions I received from people when I told them I was working on the topic of strategy. They invariably would ask, "What type of strategy?" "Are you working on military, foreign policy, or business strategy?" When I said I was writing about the concept of strategy, rather than any particular type, eyes would invariably glaze over. I concluded that in most peoples' minds, strategy is inextricably linked to particular professions, and that it is seldom thought of as a subject worthy of study in its own right. *Strategic Thinking in 3D* came from a belief that the right way to study strategy is to focus first on the broad principles of strategy, followed by an application of these principles to the peculiarities of individual professions.

Another motivation came from the belief that strategy had to be rescued as a concept. Like the Buddhist tale in which several blind men feel an elephant and, depending on which part of the animal each of them feels, go on to describe it as something completely different, strategy means different things to different people.[1] Even among professionals, there is little consensus as to what strategy actually is. The concept has become an integral part of the military, diplomatic, and business lexicons, but each of these professions uses a different language and, more fundamentally, means something different when speaking about strategy. Diplomats and statesmen, whose focus is on overarching national interests, have completely different strategic frames of reference than military commanders whose focus is on the more limited terrain of the battlefield.[2] Business executives, too, use the language of strategy. But their interpretation of the concept deviates significantly from what it means to their military and political counterparts.[3] The consequence of using the strategy terminology loosely to describe very different types of activity is that the concept has become diffused and devoid of any real clarity.

There are multiple reasons why this divide on strategy has occurred. One is the historical evolution of the concept. The notion of strategy has its antecedents in, and evolved with, the military profession. Starting with Sun Tzu—and later expanded by Carl von Clausewitz and other classical theorists—the concept of strategy took shape according to the logics of war and battle. While these classical theorists did see military strategy as serving broader political ends, their analyses were largely confined to the pursuit of military victory. Nonetheless, the concept of strategy evolved over time, extending beyond the battlefield and into the diplomatic and political arenas. In the diplomatic and political spheres, strategy took on a different form, expanding to a focus on a broad range of strategic assets including, but not limited to, instruments of force.

Business strategy has also had its own unique historical trajectory. Even though business professionals in competitive situations have traditionally borrowed insights from military strategists, the effects of globalizing industries have forced executives to expand their strategic vision beyond the narrow "business-as-war" paradigm to include something approximating the more expansive notion of grand strategy.[4] While this trend might portend eventual convergence between the business and foreign policy notions of strategy, there is little evidence today to suggest that differences in how strategy is conceptualized by national security and business professionals have been significantly narrowed.

Another factor contributing to the fuzziness of the concept is the casual way strategy has become part of the modern parlance. It is often used to describe something as prosaic as a good idea or as mundane as a simple plan of action.[5] This sloppiness extends into the professional world, where strategy is used to describe a wide range of different activities. Strategic planning in government and business is often mistaken for strategy making itself, when in fact the planning process may merely entail the allocation of resources for, and implementation of, a strategy formulated at a higher level in the organization.[6] The strategy-making process involves creativity, innovation, and change, while strategic planning tends to be less about strategy and more about operations. But in some organizations these operations get confused with, or even crowd out, the higher-level function of strategy making.

The absence of a common understanding of strategy has concrete costs. A lack of strategic capacity can become an impediment to solving some of our most dauntingly complex problems. Without innovative strategies, it may be impossible to respond effectively to such challenges as climate change, the Arab Spring, international terrorism, or an ascending China. This is true regardless of whether one is looking at these challenges through the eyes of a military, government, or business professional. The strategy imperative is not unique to a given professional field but rather is part of all human endeavors.[7]

The lack of a coherent concept of strategy also constitutes a problem because most of the significant strategic challenges we face today straddle political, commercial, and military boundaries. The challenges we faced in Iraq and continue to face in Afghanistan are examples of strategic situations that defy categorization, as they do not fit neatly into the sectors of military, diplomatic, or business.[8] The strategic problems we have faced in these two countries, and the challenges we are likely to face in the future, are multifaceted. They require better interagency coordination between the military, diplomatic, and development arms of the U.S. government, as well as between governments, NGOs, and the private sector. In other words, complex, multifaceted problems have outstripped the capacity of sector specific strategies and cry out for integrated, cross-sector strategic responses. But the lack of unanimity when it comes to strategy, coupled with conceptual sloppiness, make communication and strategic coordination across these sectors inefficient, unwieldy, and sometimes impossible. As the complexity of strategic problems grows, and challenges from nontraditional actors become more prevalent, the need for more robust cross-sector strategic approaches also grows.

Another problem created by strategic disarray has less to do with the dynamics of cooperation between the business and governmental sectors, and more to do with the nature of conflict in today's international system. The adversaries faced by governments now include, but are not limited to, traditional nation-states. Conventional strategic approaches are inadequate for governments confronting challenges from non-state actors like al-Qaeda, Somali pirates, or empowered individuals or organizations like WikiLeaks. The strategic responses that worked for contending with strong nation-state rivals are also ineffective in dealing with the asymmetric challenges that come from failing or failed states.

Similarly, global corporations find little help from traditional business strategies to guide them as they face intensified, and sometimes adversarial, interactions with governments and NGOs.

The last pragmatic reason that sector-specific strategies are inadequate has to do with the growing trend toward professionals migrating between the public and private sectors over the duration of their careers. Since sector-specific approaches to strategy are not particularly portable, this creates a large learning curve for those individuals who want to cross over to another field. These individuals need a general grounding in strategy that is transferable between the private and public sectors. While someone expertly schooled in strategy may be able to extract lessons from one field and apply them later to another, the lack of a common framework makes this difficult for most people.

A framework capable of resuscitating strategy must accomplish two things. It must apply to military, diplomatic, and business practitioners, offering tools for helping a wide range of professionals analyze, understand, and respond to the strategies of their traditional, as well as their nontraditional, adversaries. While the craft and goals—security vs. corporate profits—of the national security and military strategist are different from those of the business leader, there is a similar intellectual process that applies to and needs to imbue both cultures.

The framework must also elevate strategy to its proper level. Strategy is about adapting to or shaping one's environment so that what otherwise would be improbable becomes possible—it is about creating a multiplier effect on resources and actions. Considering strategy this way catapults it to a higher level than what is commonly referred to as strategic planning. Although good strategy involves significant planning, it is much more than that. Strategy is a high-performance function that involves creating change and generating energy on behalf of an organization's goals and objectives.

HOW TO USE THIS BOOK

Strategic Thinking in 3D attempts to respond to the strategic problems previously described by offering a general framework for thinking strategically that can be used across a wide range of public and private sector professions. The underlying assumption of an approach that can be broadly applied is that strategy embodies universal principles that transcend the traditional public-private sector boundaries. This is not to suggest that there are no significant differences in how strategy is applied or practiced between the public and private sectors. But it does argue that these differences notwithstanding, the underlying principles are fundamentally the same. Much like different languages having a common linguistic root, strategy across disciplines has common conceptual underpinnings.[9]

This book argues that regardless of whether one approaches strategy from the government or business perspectives, the common challenges are how to turn inert assets into muscular capability, as well as how to model and then make decisions within complex external environments. Since all organizations practicing strategy do so within the context of their external environments, mapping these environments and then weighing strategic options within them is critically important. Whether the organization is a business or a government, strategic success or failure is shaped by how successfully it navigates its dynamic external environments.

The premise of this book contends that for most organizations this external environment is multidimensional, and that strategic success or failure can come from how deftly the strategist thinks about and navigates these dimensions. Practicing strategy multidimensionally is like a combination of fencing and playing billiards. As in fencing, it involves directly confronting and maneuvering against the opponent. But like billiards, where the goal of pocketing one ball is achieved by hitting another, strategy involves influencing the opponent's behavior by targeting its external environment. In line with this, *Strategic Thinking in 3D* argues that strategy needs to be thought of in three-dimensional terms—systems, opponents, and groups, all of which are critical elements of an organization's strategic environment.

There are three important caveats to keep in mind when reading this book. First, the general framework is intended to be used suggestively rather than dogmatically. There are significant differences between the strategic environments of the private and public sectors, and these should not be papered over. The framework should be used to tease out insights about an organization's external environment, but one's view of the environment should not be artificially forced to fit the framework.

Strategy and strategic environments are messy, chaotic, and resistant to any rigid and overly simplified approach. The book is designed to help decision makers think their way through the fog of uncertainty in their external environments. The concepts should not be abused through an overly rigid or dogmatic application; the framework should be thought of as a guide for thinking about the complexities of strategy, rather than as a manual to be mechanically followed.

The second caveat is that the book intentionally takes a broad horizontal, as opposed to a deep vertical, approach to the concept of strategy. There is already an abundance of literature that focuses on the different levels of strategy and the vertical links between strategy, operations, and tactics.[10] While *Strategic Thinking in 3D* occasionally touches on those subjects, the book focuses on an area that is underdeveloped in the literature: how organizations across a wide expanse of professions can map, model, and then develop strategies within their external environments. It is in this broad, horizontal domain that many of the insights into the common elements of strategy emerge. It is also within this domain that some of the most critical strategic thinking needs to be done, and it is where the importance of an interdisciplinary approach to strategy reveals itself. In this way, *Strategic Thinking in 3D* is about getting national security, foreign policy, and business professionals to think more strategically within their respective environments, rather than how strategy gets operationalized within each of these contexts.

The third caveat is that while the book provides plenty of information for readers focused on problems for which there are no obvious opponents, the case studies are largely drawn from situations involving enemies and competitors. This comes from several biases. The first is that many of the challenges we face today, like the rise of China, extremism in the Middle East, and international terrorism, involve a specific adversary. The second is that even strategies that don't focus on a specific adversary, but instead target a problem like poverty reduction and climate change, provoke responses from detractors who aim to undermine the strategy or mission. Any focus on strategy then needs to take into account other actors and possible opponents. Thus, this books tilts heavily in the area of competitive strategy.

The chapters that follow methodically develop the concept of a general approach to strategic thinking. The introduction addresses the question of definitions and assumptions. Before wading into the deep waters of how to think strategically, we first need to grapple with the challenge of how to define the concept. Much like looking through a kaleidoscope, strategy is defined and examined from different angles, using an internal as well as an external lens. Moving beyond the definitional question, we then delve into the underlying assumptions or logics behind strategy. While the definitions help us establish the boundaries of strategy, the logics help us gain a deeper understanding of the concept and its animating principles.

Chapter 1 addresses the importance of setting goals in strategy. It explores the question of how to set actionable strategic goals and makes the important distinction between primary goals, subsidiary goals, and milestone goals. Chapter 2 then transitions into the question of strategic resources and capability, emphasizing how the transformation of an organization's inert assets into dynamic and muscular capabilities is a sine qua non for successful strategies. Since capability contributes to the multiplier effect that is so important for strategy, the process of manufacturing capability needs to be a central focus.

Chapter 3 introduces strategies in the dimension of systems—the first of the three dimensions. This chapter examines how organizations can indirectly build their competitive advantage by shaping the context within which battles with their opponent take place. It addresses why creating sustainable competitive advantages requires generating leverage within this context. The chapter will focus on the challenge of applying pressure to the opponent by altering the external environment it relies on for sustaining its leverage and power.

Chapter 4 deals with strategies in the dimension of opponents. An important dimension of strategy obviously involves the dynamic of direct competition. Here the strategist must be skilled at maneuvering around competitors, enemies, and allies. This chapter covers how to analyze a competitor's capability—its motivation and strategy—and then use this analysis to assess one's own competitive challenges. This chapter also looks at how to weigh strategic options given one's competitive position. Whereas chapter 3 focused on indirectly challenging the adversary by shaping its context and eroding its leverage, chapter 4 emphasizes directly confronting the adversary and exploiting the leverage and competitive advantage that have been created.

Chapter 5 discusses strategies in the dimension of groups. Like system strategies, these too are indirect strategies that aim to compromise the leverage of the adversary. The realm of groups for businesses consists of consumer groups, market segments, and other stakeholders, while for foreign policy practitioners it is composed of mass-publics and influential institutions. For foreign policy strategy this dimension involves public diplomacy targeted toward groups at home and abroad, while for business strategy it takes the form of market segmentation and corporate social responsibility. This chapter covers the skills of identifying and analyzing formal and informal groups. Strategy here involves creating, segmenting, and mobilizing large groups for the purpose of creating competitive and strategic advantage.

Chapter 6 illustrates the power of looking at strategy in three dimensions by using the case of al-Qaeda's strategy against the United States. This chapter brings together the concepts developed in earlier chapters and demonstrates how strategic success often comes from the cascading effect of "wins" in all three of these dimensions. Conversely, strategic failure can come from the mutual reinforcement of "losses" across these same three dimensions. Through reinforcement and integration of the concepts, the reader will see how strategy in 3D actually works.

The conclusion provides final insights about strategy and encapsulates the lessons learned throughout the book. It also summarizes the key steps in the strategy process, so that a business or national security professional could refer to this chapter for a refresher of the concepts and steps outlined in the book.

ACKNOWLEDGMENTS

No author deserves 100 percent of the credit for a book. Certainly I benefited greatly from others kind enough to share their thoughts through their own work, as well as through comments on my work. First I have to thank the members of the Teaching Strategy Group at the U.S. Army War College for their intellectual support for this project, as well as for serving as an incredible intellectual powerhouse on the subject of strategy.

While too numerous to mention them all, there are a few individuals who deserve to be singled out. Gabriel Marcella has served as the lead person of the group, as well as the primary author of an edited volume on strategy, *Teaching Strategy: Challenge and Response* (Carlisle, PA: Strategic Studies Institute, 2010), to which I contributed. Gabriel always made himself available for musings about strategy, and he is a much-valued friend and kindred soul on our favorite shared subject. Rich Yarger, too, deserves specific mention. Rich, an accomplished scholar of strategy in his own right, read through the entire manuscript and provided invaluable comments. And Thomaz da Costa from the National Defense University has always provided the much-needed spark to our discussions about strategy.

At Georgetown University, which has been my intellectual home for the past eight years, there are also folks that need to be mentioned. Chester Crocker, the James R. Schlesinger Professor of Strategic Studies at Georgetown and former assistant secretary of state, has been an incredible friend and sounding board on matters relating to strategy. Special mention also goes to my students in MSFS 597 (Strategy: Security, Development and Business) in the spring semesters of 2010, 2011, and 2012. The graduate seminar served as a crucible for the ideas developed in this book, and the students served as a great sounding board for ideas both worthy and those not-so-worthy. I also want to thank my student assistant from the University of Pittsburgh, Helen Ewing, for the work she did researching and analyzing al-Qaeda's communication strategy.

Finally, my loving family has been an amazing support system throughout the book. My wife, Mahnaz, was always there for me throughout this process, and my adult children, Arash and Hermine, were always there to bring me down to earth and provide much-needed distraction when I took my work on strategy too seriously. And my mother, Mary Harrison, certainly deserves credit for leading by example of how one develops strategies for survival in the face of adversity. These credits notwithstanding, all the blame for any failings in this book should redound to me.

INTRODUCTION: DEMYSTIFYING STRATEGY

There are skeptics who question whether robust strategy in the twenty-first century is actually possible. Some would argue that we are facing a paradox—the problems of today make the need for strategy more urgent, but the complexity of these problems has outstripped our capacity to respond strategically.[1] While the challenges governments and businesses face today are clearly more daunting than ever before, they are neither insuperable nor resistant to strategic solutions. The bar has certainly been raised by the nature of the problems we face, but it would be imprudent to give up on strategy. Instead we need to strengthen our strategic capacity and improve our strategic paradigms.

Strategy can be an enigmatic concept. One of the keys to making it less mysterious is defining what strategy is, as well as teasing out what assumptions it makes. By addressing these issues, we can provide a platform for professionals who want to hone their strategic thinking skills.[2]

WHAT IS STRATEGY?

The problem with defining strategy isn't a shortage of definitions; there are many, but most are inadequate or incomplete. Anyone looking for one silver-bullet definition that accurately captures the general concept in a way that applies across disciplines will be sorely disappointed. The national security and business professions boast their own theorists who define strategy, but in ways that are relevant only to their respective fields.

The problem is compounded by the fact that within each of the professions there is little in the way of agreement about how strategy should be defined. Some might argue that this is not intrinsically problematic, citing the fact that most academic disciplines thrive in spite of, or even because of, significant debates over definitions, theories, and concepts. But this is less true with the more practical field of strategy, where the upshot of scholars talking past one another, rather than to one another, is that professionals are left to pick through the clutter of definitions on their own, hoping to find something useful.

One question that needs to be asked is whether a single, universal definition of strategy is necessary to make the concept clear for the practitioner—one that is equally useful to military, foreign policy, and business strategists? Or, should practitioners deepen their understanding of what strategy is by looking at it through multiple definitional lenses?

I would argue that the answer to both of these questions is yes. For professionals who want to sharpen their strategic thinking skills, there are immense benefits to having one, overarching definition to ground their understanding. But there are also benefits to looking at strategy from a number of different perspectives.

Since a single definition provides the benefits of simplicity and clarity, and multiple definitions provide granularity and depth, I have tried to provide the best of both. The universal definition is broad enough to encompass the others, while the individual definitions provide unique insights that deepen the general concept. Think of it as the mental equivalent of looking at an object through a kaleidoscope. As the device is twisted and the angles change, the viewer sees the same object in new and different ways. Looking at strategy from various definitional angles and vantage points will help us capture its essence.

Before we start down the path of defining strategy, the practitioner needs to understand that strategy has both an inward and outward face, meaning it takes place both inside and outside an organization or country. The inward face of strategy involves setting goals, building muscular capability, and generating the energy. It takes place within, and under the control of, an organization or country. The outward face of strategy involves flexing this muscular capability, expending the energy, and taking action in the external environment.[3] It takes place outside the control of an organization or country.

A SINGLE UMBRELLA DEFINITION

Andrew F. Krepinevich and Barry D. Watts offer one of the best overarching, universally applicable definitions I have found. According to them, "Strategy is fundamentally about identifying or creating asymmetric advantages that can be exploited to help achieve one's ultimate objectives despite resource and other constraints, most importantly the opposing efforts of adversaries or competitors and the inherent unpredictability of strategic outcomes."[4]

This high level definition captures both the inward and outward faces of strategy. It creates an understanding that strategy involves overcoming challenges that come from both inside and outside an organization. The focus on resource constraints and the need to create asymmetric advantages or capabilities points us toward some of the internal challenges faced when preparing and executing strategy. The focus on exploiting advantages against adversaries and competitors, and the unpredictability of strategic outcomes addresses the external challenges strategy needs to overcome.

The utility of this definition is that it is not limited to any field of study or practice. While there are many differences in how strategies are formulated by countries, governments, and businesses, there are also many similarities. In order to craft a strategy, countries and businesses need to internally leverage resources to create capability advantages before they can launch their strategies externally. Businesses and governments also need to contend with adversaries and unpredictability in their external environments in order to meet their strategic goals. In doing so, they need to overcome significant internal resource constraints and limits imposed by the external environment.

There are, however, limits to what this single umbrella definition can do. Although it tells the practitioner what strategy is, the umbrella definition does not provide much practical on-the-ground guidance to any particular country or business. It captures the breadth of strategy but is less useful when trying to understand the depth of the concept. No single definition can adequately capture both the depth and breadth of strategy.

A DEFINITIONAL KALEIDOSCOPE

The purpose of the definitional kaleidoscope is to provide more depth by picking up where the umbrella definition leaves off. It will encompass definitions that give us a view into the inward face of strategy, as well as definitions that give us a perspective onto strategy's outward face.

Inward-Focused Definitions

Using an internal lens to define strategy provides much-needed insights into the importance of leveraging resources, decision making, and processes. Strategy is about creating a multiplier effect on resources, making mutually reinforcing decisions, and developing processes that can propel organizations beyond the realities of today to the desired futures of tomorrow. Since all of these originate inside an organization, inwardly focused definitions, like those addressed in the following, are critically important. Definitions of strategy using an inward perspective can be categorized according to their particular area of focus. Let's examine each of these categories in turn.

Definition Type 1:
Strategy as the Leveraging of Resources

Resources are the fuel for strategy and the ingredients that go into making strategic capability. But it is important not to fall into the tempting trap of defining strategy as merely the mechanical function of resource allocation and budgeting. The following are several definitions that highlight both the perils and the benefits of defining strategy in terms of resource allocation. We will also examine the utility of defining strategy more robustly to reflect the way in which resources are used to their best advantage and to create organizational capability.

The Resource Trap

One of the most widely referenced definitions of strategy in U.S. Army circles is the "three-legged stool" model developed by military strategist Art Lykke, who defined it as the "calculated relationship between ends, ways, and means." Ends are the goals to be achieved, ways represent how these objectives will be met, and means are the resources available for achieving these goals. Lykke's central argument is that an imbalance between resources and goals causes the three-legged stool to wobble, the upshot being an increased risk that the strategy will fail. While Lykke doesn't refute that large goals can be achieved with disproportionally small resources, his work implies that the essence of strategy is the calibration of, and balancing between, ends (goals) and means (resources).[5]

Lykke's model is elegant in its simplicity and easily adaptable to governments, businesses, and non-state actors. By connecting the dots between ends, ways, and means, Lykke makes an important contribution to distilling strategy down to three basic moving parts. But the strength of his model is also its weakness. The danger of the Lykke model is that its literal interpretation can lead to the demotion, rather than elevation, of strategy. Instead of pushing practitioners to see strategy as the potential to make possible what might otherwise be improbable, the Lykke model could lead them to conclude that strategy is mechanical, linear, and pedestrian. Many of the strategic situations that business and foreign policy professionals face involve trying to achieve outsized goals with a dwindling set of resources. Following a Lykke approach could lure the strategy professional away from seeing strategy as the art of achieving more with less, and closer to a depiction of strategy as the mere balancing between resources and goals.[6]

One of Lykke's strengths is that he forces us to focus on the relationship between strategy and risk. Unfortunately what he concludes about this relationship could lead the practitioner down the wrong path. Lykke argues that if goals aren't properly calibrated to resources, the risk of strategic failure increases significantly, but he tends to underplay situations in which the opportunities justify the risk. In fact one could argue that true strategy comes into play, not when there is symmetry between resources and goals, but rather when there is asymmetry. True strategy involves figuring ways to build a bridge between small means and large ends, thus converting risk into opportunity.

More Robust Definitions

What the practitioner needs are definitions of strategy that use a resource lens but portray it as a high level, dynamic concept, rather than as static and prosaic. Strategy should reflect the amplification, not just the allocation, of resources.

Historian John Gaddis's definition, which builds on Lykke's, is quite useful to the professional in this regard. He argues that strategy is "the calculated relationship of means to *large* ends."[7] Unlike Lykke, whose focus is on the risk incurred when there is a gap between means and ends, Gaddis suggests that strategy is the bridge that enables that gap to close. Strategy is what makes outsized goals possible, despite an asymmetry between these goals and available resources.[8] Similarly Richard Betts, in his path-breaking work on strategy, argues that "strategy is most important when it provides added value to resources, [and] functions as a force multiplier."[9]

We can look at Gaddis's and Betts's argument, then, as a kind of rejoinder to the Lykke model. Strategies involving large ends but proportionally smaller means may not necessarily be fraught with significantly higher levels of risk than strategies where there is a greater balance between the two. It is the quality of the strategy, not solely the numeric relationship between means and ends, which determines the degree of risk and the probability of success or failure. Strategy is about calculating, overcoming, and managing the risk that comes from using proportionally smaller resources to achieve outsized results.

Definition Type 2:
Strategy as a Set of Mutually Reinforcing Decisions

Definitions of strategy based on decision-making complement the resource-based definitions discussed in the previous section. Juxtaposing these two types of definitions can be useful to practitioners because it forces them to focus on the resources needed for a particular strategy, as well as the decisions needed about how to convert these resources into capability.

There are two different levels at which the practitioner should be thinking about strategy in terms of decision making. The first is that strategy involves deciding which of several possible paths is most likely to lead to the fulfillment of the goals and interests of the country or business. At this level, strategy is about making a single, discrete decision that will determine the direction of the government or business.

The second level comes into play when the strategist is shaping the decision-making pattern, not just making one particular decision. Strategy doesn't end after a major decision has been made—a series of follow-on decisions will also need to be made that support that direction. At this level strategy involves making sure that these decisions mutually reinforce, rather than work against, one another. This leads us to define strategy as "a set or pattern of mutually reinforcing decisions that taken together propel an organization or country towards its goals." The multiplier effect of strategy comes about from the compounding effect of these decisions.[10]

The Limits of Equating Strategy with Decision Making

But one shouldn't get too comfortable with distilling the abstract concept of strategy down to the more manageable concept of decision making. Management guru Harry Mintzberg cautions us against assuming that strategy is all about deliberate decision making. He argues that strategies in organizations can originate from many sources and take multiple forms. While strategies can be deliberate, meaning they begin with a decision at the top of the organization, they can also emerge incrementally in response to previous decisions, institutional culture, and external environments.[11]

Leaders may decide to move their organizations or countries off of the arc set in motion by previous decisions. However they will often find it more prudent and beneficial to lean into, rather than try to change, this previously determined direction. This is particularly true of countries or businesses whose leaders lack the latitude or support necessary to move in a completely new direction. This shouldn't be construed as the country or business being rudderless or bereft of a strategy, as long as it is on an identifiable path, and is sufficiently responsive and adaptive to changes in its environment.

Strategies can emerge organically, as opposed to deliberately, as organizations adapt to challenges imposed by their external environments. Leaders need to be aware of their capacity for making deliberate strategic decisions. But they should also be alert to the emergent strategic patterns in their organizations that both enable and constrain them.[12]

Definition Type 3: Strategy as Process

Defining strategy in terms of process also provides interesting insights into the concept. J. C. Wiley defines strategy as "a plan of action designed in order to achieve some end; a purpose together with a system of measures for its accomplishment."[13] Process-oriented definitions of strategy, like Wiley's, focus our attention less on one central decision and more on strategy as a sustained effort over time. While defining strategy in process terms doesn't contradict a decision-making approach, it does force the practitioner to look beyond a central decision and to focus on how that decision gets implemented. It focuses on risk assessment, resource management, and the measures and feedback loops required to sustain major strategic decisions. In addition to decision making, strategy requires continuous adaptation to changes in the external environment, including changes that occur naturally and those that result from earlier strategic decisions. Strategy must be iterative, dynamic, and process focused in order to meet these challenges.

Outward-Focused Definitions

As necessary as an inward view of strategy is, it is insufficient by itself. While the energy and propulsion of strategy is generated internally, success or failure is determined in the external environment.

Several outwardly focused definitions are useful for the practitioner. The first depicts strategy as managing uncertainty and risk in the external environment. The second emphasizes maneuvering to create competitive advantage against opponents in the external environment. The third portrays strategy as the act of shaping the external environment to further one's goals. Each of these definitions gives us a slightly different view of strategy's outward face.

Definition Type 1: Strategy as Managing Uncertainty and Risk

Whether the organization is a government or a business, strategy takes place in a dynamic and uncertain external environment. Success or failure hinges on how well one accounts for and adapts to change and uncertainty in that environment. Thinking about strategy in terms of managing risk and controlling uncertainty is critically important for any serious professional, and any fulsome treatment of strategy has to capture this relationship.

One of the more interesting definitions in this regard is offered by American diplomat Charles W. "Chas" Freeman Jr., who defines strategy as "the effort to gain and retain the initiative, and to minimize the effects of chance."[14] Strategy, according to Freeman, involves seizing control over the situation, such that risk and the effects of chance are mitigated. His definition also points to the fact that strategy and risk are inextricably linked. While it is impossible, and even undesirable, to eliminate risk entirely, strategy involves taking and retaining the initiative over opponents, enemies, and competitors to minimize risk. In other words, strategy can be thought of as the art of identifying and capitalizing on opportunity while managing the attendant risk.

But what if the environment can't be harnessed, controlled, or shaped? Military historians Mark Grimsley and Williamson Murray provide a counterpoint to Freeman. They argue that "strategy is a process, a constant adaptation to shifting conditions and circumstances in a world where chance, uncertainty and ambiguity dominate."[15] Whereas Freeman implies that strategy involves controlling and shaping the environment such that risk can be significantly limited, Grimsley and Murray see strategy more as adapting to an environment in which high levels of risk are inevitable and can merely be mitigated or managed. Strategy, according to their portrayal, involves maneuvering around a relatively risky environment rather than trying to change it. Their portrayal is useful to the strategist who might not be in the position of gaining and retaining the initiative.

Definition Type 2: Strategy as Competing

Definitions that force us to look at strategy through the lens of competition can complement the more abstract notion of strategy as risk management. Part of the risk faced by the strategist is the uncertainty surrounding an opponent's motives, capabilities, and strategy.

One of the most insightful definitions that encapsulate this school of thought is provided by the French general and military strategist André Beaufre, who argues that strategy "is the art of the dialectic between two opposing wills, using force to resolve their disputes."[16] In other words, strategy entails the interaction between two (or more) opponents. According to Beaufre, and in contrast to Lykke, strategy is energetic, dynamic, and interactive. It is not a static, abstract, or sterile process, but instead involves a back-and-forth jostling for competitive advantage. While the battle between adversaries may originate with a well-planned decision that takes possible risk factors into account, once the opening gambit is made, strategy becomes a battle of wits, force, and maneuver in an environment of uncertainty.

For Beaufre, the strategist needs to be a contemplative decision maker and risk manager, as well as a swift, agile fighter who can adapt to the response of an enemy who gets a "say" in the outcome.

Definition Type 3: Strategy as Shaping the External Environment

Not all strategy involves direct interaction with an opponent or competitor. Strategy can also involve interaction with the broader external environment. Companies, for example, can plot strategies to shape the structure of their industries, and countries may try to shape the structure of regional or international political or economic systems. Any typology of definitions designed to be useful to the practitioner needs to capture this angle.

Strategy involves the shaping of, or adaptation to, an organization's external environment on behalf of its goals. While any view of the external environment will include individual opponents or competitors that happen to impede one's goals, defining strategy this way forces us to look at the broader context within which competition takes place. That context may include an opponent's allies and enemies, or the system within which relationships with these actors take place. It also forces the strategist to consider how an opponent's positioning within the external environment affects its power, leverage, and competitive advantage. The goal of strategy is to shape the structure of the environment, such that one's opponent is forced into a disadvantaged competitive position.

THE ASSUMPTIONS OF STRATEGY

Definitions give us the breadth and scope of strategy. But to give greater texture to what strategy means for the professional, we need to tease out its underlying assumptions.[17]

The Assumption of Interests

Although ancient Chinese strategist Sun Tzu and the Prussian military strategist Clausewitz are properly credited with developing the concept of strategy, strategy is inherent to human nature. So what about human nature gives life to strategy? As individuals, our behavior is largely driven by the fulfillment of needs, the most basic of which relate to subsistence, like nourishment and shelter. But humans also have higher-level needs, such as self-esteem and self-realization.[18] Individuals adapt their behavior to increase their chances of meeting these needs in an environment of scarcity and adversity.

Businesses, countries, and other organizations behave similarly. They have institutional needs, called interests, which animate their behavior and drive the need for strategy. Like individuals, governments and businesses adapt their behaviors to increase the likelihood that their interests will be protected or fulfilled. This behavior of adapting, and in some cases shaping, in the pursuit of interests is what gives rise to strategy. Without these interests, there would be little need for strategy.

But what else about the pursuit of interests drives the need for strategy? While some interests might be fulfilled without any opposition, there are generally obstacles, challengers, and enemies whose interests conflict with yours. One way to think about strategy is that it provides a road map for protecting or pursuing interests in the face of adversity.[19]

The Assumption of Opposing Wills

Closely related to the logic of interests is the logic of opposing wills.[20] While the logic of interests reveals to us strategy's purpose, the logic of opposing wills reveals its challenge. The strategic imperative exists because there are others who will try to prevent you from fulfilling your interests. One could argue that in the absence of opponents, interests could be fulfilled without a strategy. The need for strategy arises because there is likely to be conflict between your interests and an opponent's. A strategy needs to be devised to improve your chances of prevailing over the opponent's challenges to these interests.

The Assumption of Choice

In the absence of choice, strategy doesn't exist. Seldom is the strategist presented with an unlimited number of choices, but strategy presupposes the availability of some choice. While strategy can be used to expand the number of options available, and in some cases can actually create options where none exist, it generally involves choosing among alternative paths of action.

Generally strategy has little meaning in situations where only one possible course of action exists. Companies with insufficient cash flows may have no alternative other than bankruptcy. While the company still has to make operational and tactical decisions, the absence of real options other than bankruptcy means that the business is operating outside the realm of strategy. This could also be true in the case of a government that has just been resoundingly defeated. In the immediate aftermath of World War II, Germany, having little in the way of choice, operated for a short time outside the realm of strategy.

We should be cautious, however, about pushing the logic of choice too far. It shouldn't cause us to conclude that strategy requires limitless options. While they typically have a wider range of options than their weaker counterparts, powerful actors still operate under constraints. These constraints may be internally driven, like resource limits or constitutional strictures, or they can be externally driven, imposed by the actions of an opponent. But whether the range of available options is wide or narrow, the presence of some choice gives meaning to the possibility of strategy.

The Assumption of Limits

Ponder for a moment what strategy would mean in a utopian world where time, resources, and space were limitless. Would strategy even be relevant? Think about the strategic challenges of today. Apple is competing for discretionary consumer dollars in a difficult economic climate. A dollar of revenue from consumer spending in Apple's coffers means one less for Samsung, Motorola, Dell, or HP. Apple needs a clearly defined and compelling strategy to compete successfully with these companies. What would it mean strategically for Apple if, in a utopian world, consumer discretionary income was suddenly unlimited? While the company would still need to offer compelling products and have a strong brand to get noticed by consumers, its value proposition and strategy would not need to be as finely honed as it does in the real world, where consumers are forced to make spending choices.

But since we don't live in a utopian world, let's look at how strategy operates on a premise of limits of space, time, and resources. First, it assumes that space is limited. Strategy doesn't exist in a physical vacuum; rather it takes place in a territorial dimension—a world where competition for space is a zero-sum game. This dimension may entail a piece of geography mutually coveted by two contending parties, like the Taliban and Afghan government. Or it could be the vying for a dominant share of particular geographic markets by Apple and Dell. Strategy in each of these cases involves how to improve one's position or gain control over these limited geographic terrains.

Strategy also rests on the logic of limited time. In the everyday world, time proceeds at a constant pace. But in the mysterious world of strategy, the pace of time can be variable, meaning it can speed up or slow down. To make matters even more complicated, time can proceed faster for one party in a conflict than for the other. How does this make sense? For the strategist, time moves according to the pace of change in the external environment and according to constraints imposed by the internal environment. A company making cement operates according to a different speed than a company making computers, since the pace at which the computer company has to respond to its strategic environment is much faster than the required response time of the cement company. Because the pace of technological innovation coming from competition is much more rapid in the electronics industry than it is in the relatively lethargic building products industry, the challenges of innovation and the imperatives for change are much greater.

On the national security front, does the strategic clock in Afghanistan move at the same pace for the United States as it does for our enemies? One could argue that the clock that drives the resistance is slower than the clock that drives the United States. There are both internal and external factors that account for this. The first factor is external—the United States is in the defensive position and is forced to respond to the moves of the enemy. The second factor is internal—it corresponds with the impatience of the American people relative to the war and the looming U.S. election cycles. Since these constraints don't operate on our enemies, we can argue that they have time on their side. In a way, this allows time to move slower for our enemies, as they can wait out the situation, delaying the gratification of success until U.S. forces leave Afghanistan.

Strategy is also animated by the logic of limited resources. Back to the notion of a utopian world, if resources were unlimited, the imperative for strategy would be less. It is the need to bridge the gap between finite resources and ambitious goals that creates the demand for strategy. In fact, the logic of limited resources is also related to the logic of limited time. Tight constraints on resources will impinge on time and make the strategic clock tick faster. A small company with limited financial and human resources will generally have a narrower window of time to show success than a larger company with deeper pockets. The smaller company will be racing against time because its financial resources may run out before its strategy gains traction. Similarly, a small country in a military battle with a larger foe may be operating according to a faster-ticking strategic clock. The key will be to show success before its larger adversary gets the opportunity to destroy the country's military and financial resources. Conversely, larger adversaries with deeper resources may operate according to a slower-ticking strategic clock. Their greater margin for error and deeper resources mean that they may have a more time than their resource-strapped adversary. But whether for small actors with scarce resources or larger actors with greater resources, strategy has meaning within the context of the logic of resource limits.

The Assumption of Passion

The logics of interests, choice, and limits speak to the rational side of strategy. These assume that strategy is animated by rational impulses and calculations. But strategy also has a side governed by passion. While states and businesses may pursue objective interests and goals, rationality alone does not fully explain the fervor with which states and businesses prosecute their strategies. Even though government or business leaders set goals according to a rational calculation of interests, their citizens, soldiers and employees may rally behind them simply because of a passionate devotion to the country or the company's brand. Clausewitz understood the role passion plays in strategy, suggesting that fervent support by the people is a requisite ingredient to success in war and strategy. In addition to the calculations of the leader, and the courage and creativity of the commander, the passion of the people shapes the nature of war and strategy.[21] No doubt there are also cases where the leadership itself has been characterized by irrational fervor, as in the Japanese decision to attack Pearl Harbor.[22] While strategy may rest on a foundation of objective logics of interests, choices, and limits, its pursuit is often animated by base human emotions.

The Assumption of Integration

The assumption of integration is another defining principal of strategy. There are two types of integration that are important to the concept of strategy, one inward and the other outward. Strategy is built on an assumption that states and businesses can act purposefully and coordinate their resources and actions on behalf of a goal. Military strategic thinker Colin Gray's analysis of strategy makes a strong contribution here. He argues that strategy requires unlike functions to be bridged, something that is neither natural nor easy.[23] But easy to achieve or not, the integration of internal effort is a sine qua non for strategy. Functions that are differentiated in an organization must be integrated and marshaled on behalf of a common strategic purpose.

Strategy is also built on an assumption that the external world has patterns of integration. As chaotic and disorganized as markets and international political systems may be, the strategist's job is to tease out the patterns of integration, which can be very subtle. Companies develop hypotheses to predict how markets and industries behave in an integrated, patterned fashion. These insights provide the basis for their corporate strategies. Foreign policy strategists also have to correctly analyze the interactive dynamics of the international system in order to develop appropriate strategic moves.[24] For example, an understanding of the undercurrents and patterns that connect the uprisings in Egypt, Tunisia, Syria, and Libya is required for a strategist working on U.S. policy towards the Middle East. Without connections and integration between events, processes, people, and things, strategy would be less relevant.

The Assumption of Causality

The assumption of causality is related to the assumption of integration.[25] Harry Yarger sums it up when he argues that strategy assumes there is the potential to "create more favorable outcomes than might otherwise exist if left to chance or in the hand of others."[26] Though not all consequences of action can be controlled or predicted, strategy rests on the assumption that actions can make a difference. It involves developing theories about how actions have a causal connection to outcomes, how the world works, and about the first and second order effects of particular actions and decisions.

While strategists have to believe in a causal relationship between actions and outcomes to carry on with their work, they should also be cautious about the ability to predict or even control those outcomes. Richard Betts cautions us against imputing too much causality between actions and outcomes. In his provocative article "Is Strategy an Illusion?" he argues that though a central tenet of strategy is causality, we should be sensitive to the limits of predicting how actions will produce particular outcomes. He warns that even imputing outcomes that have already occurred to previous actions is dicey.[27]

But Betts doesn't dispute the fact that causality is an underlying assumption of strategy. His argument is that in an increasingly chaotic and complex world, it is difficult to predict or prove that specific strategic actions produce particular outcomes. How do we know, for example, what caused the Soviet Union to collapse? Analysts might reasonably say that actions on the part of the Reagan administration pushed the Soviet Union over the tipping point towards collapse. But just because actions by the United States correlated with the empire's collapse doesn't prove there is a causal relationship. The collapse may have been partially catalyzed by the actions of the United States but most certainly originated in the overextension and internal decay of the Soviet Union. Betts's message isn't that this kind of ambiguity means we should give up on strategy; it is just that we should be careful not to overplay our hand by assuming that we can predict what outcomes our actions will produce.

The Assumption of Leverage

Strategy involves getting countries, businesses, leaders, and consumers to behave in ways they might not otherwise. This requires leverage, which is the potential of one actor to exert influence over the actions of another. How should the strategist be thinking about leverage? It is important to remember that leverage is a relative concept. If someone asks about the power profile or properties of a state, an objective answer can be provided by pointing to military, economic, and political indicators. But if someone asks how much leverage that same state has, the rejoinder needs to be: relative to whom? Leverage, as the potential to influence the behavior of another party, only has meaning within the context of a relationship with that party. How much leverage a country or business has will vary according to who the other party is. So the relationship between leverage and strategy is that strategy involves the manufacturing and exploitation of leverage.[28]

CONCLUSION

The introduction dealt with two fundamental questions about strategy: what is it and what are its underlying assumptions? We first looked at a single high-level umbrella definition, and then expanded that using the definitional kaleidoscope, which allowed us to peer at the concept from different angles.

But becoming a strategy practitioner requires more than just understanding what strategy is—it also requires a more granular comprehension of strategy. The treatment of the assumptions of strategy is intended as a deep dive into our understanding of the concept. Taken together, the definitions and assumptions should give the foreign policy and business professional a firm grounding in strategy, helping to lift the shroud of mystery that has settled over the concept.

PART 1

THE INWARD FACE OF STRATEGY

1 SETTING STRATEGIC GOALS

In the absence of goals, strategy is meaningless. Goals give strategy purpose and direction. The purpose of strategies is to create a desired outcome, or in some cases prevent an undesired outcome, and a goal is a clear representation of what that outcome is. Without clearly articulated goals, there is no way to know if a strategy has succeeded or failed, and it will also be difficult to distinguish flurries of activity from strategy. While goals may be adjusted once the strategy gets under way, this doesn't obviate the need to clearly articulate them in advance.

The goals of a strategy may be expressed in either vague or very specific terms. They may be ambitious, like winning a war against an enemy country, or transforming a lesser-known corporate brand into the industry's dominant brand. Or the goals can be of a more modest nature, like merely getting two parties in a conflict to sit down to talk, or improving a company's customer service. What is more important than the scope of the goals is that they get established and are clear.

As with much of strategy, setting goals requires being able to work simultaneously at multiple levels, as well as having an understanding of the higher-level interests that provide the context for goals. This chapter will also show why setting goals requires an understanding of how high-level primary goals tie in with lower-level subsidiary goals, and necessitates working simultaneously in the present, the future, and, through milestone goals, the intermediate future.

SETTING GOALS IN CONTEXT: CAPABILITY AND INTERESTS

At first glance setting strategic goals might appear to be a straightforward exercise and the easy part of strategy. But establishing goals is actually one of the more difficult and critical parts of the strategy-making process, and it is anything but mundane. Done properly, setting goals should entail intense debate about what a government, institution, or business has the capacity to do, and what its interests are. Goals that are set without proper regard for capability run a high risk of not being met. And while goals set without regard for interests may be met, they nevertheless run the risk of producing strategic failure.

Let's first address the issue of goals being set within the context of capability. Capability is an attribute or strength that allows a government, business, or organization to take particular types of actions. Here is an example from the national security front to demonstrate the importance of capability to the setting of goals.

Assume you work for the Israeli Foreign Ministry and are responsible for setting its strategy for Iran. Israel has been quite vocal about its belief that Iran's nuclear enrichment program potentially poses an existential threat to the country. You are tasked with determining how to deal with this problem. How would you determine which goals fit within the context of Israel's capability? Would destroying Iran's nascent nuclear enrichment program be a plausible goal, given Israel's capabilities? Would preventing Iran from advancing its current enrichment program toward weapons grade uranium be a more viable goal? Or, assuming Iran has already developed a nuclear weapon, would deterring Iran from using its weapon be a more realistic goal?

Let's briefly examine which capabilities are required for each of these different goals. Destroying or damaging Iran's nuclear program would require the capability to sustain a prolonged military engagement. Given the serious questions about Israel's ability to sustain a protracted conflict with Iran, and its ability to contain the conflict once it commences, it is questionable whether Israel has the capability to attain this goal. Preventing Iran from advancing its current uranium enrichment program may also be problematic and achieving this goal may require a repertoire of diplomatic and economic capabilities Israel doesn't have. Unless it was able to leverage its relationship with the United States, or convince the Iranians that an air strike was imminent, it is unlikely that Israel has the capability to prevent Iran from advancing its enrichment program toward producing weapons grade uranium.[1]

The question is, does Israel have the capability to deter Iran if it acquires a nuclear weapon? It appears as if a deterrence goal is realistic, given Israel's own nuclear weapons capability, its alliance with the United

States, and its much vaunted intelligence capabilities. While Israeli policymakers are unlikely to publicize their real strategic goals for Iran, their deliberations on setting goals are probably taking place within the context of the country's capabilities.

In addition to factoring in capability, the strategist needs to make sure that strategic goals are aligned with and advance an organization's interests. Technically speaking, a strategy has been successful if it achieves the goals that have been established for it. Goals are the end-states that a country or business seeks to achieve with its strategy. But achieving that goal is strategically beneficial only if it advances the interests of the organization.[2] Unless goals align with interests, their achievement may produce tactical success but lead to strategic failure.

What is the difference, then, between interests and goals? Interests are generally what an organization or country believes it needs to protect, create, or promote in order to ensure its well-being and survival. Common core interests for a country are security, legitimacy, sovereignty, and prosperity, while for a business they are sustainability, return on capital, and profitability.[3] Interests tend to be enduring, meaning they have no specific timeframe attached. In contrast to interests, goals tend to be more specific and involve a specified timeframe. For a company, a goal of selling more of a product within a given timeframe should serve the longer-term interests of sustainable growth and profitability. If achieving the revenue goal hurts the company's long-term profitability interests, then the goal hasn't been set properly. In sum, the achievement of goals should advance an organization's interests, but the two concepts are not the same thing. While goals spell out what constitutes immediate success of a strategy, interests point us toward what that success means for the organization over the long haul.

It is instructive for the practitioner to consider a case where a strategy measured solely using the criteria of goals would be deemed a success, but when measured against the higher bar of advancing the country's interests would likely be considered an abject failure. An example of this might be the U.S. military engagement in Iraq, which commenced in 2003. In a post 9/11 environment, when the perceived threat was high, the overriding core interests of the United States were national security and protection of the homeland. What were the goals that initially guided the strategy of the Bush administration in Iraq? In 2003, the most immediate goal for Iraq was the toppling of Saddam

Hussein's regime. There were other goals as well, such as discovery and elimination of weapons of mass destruction, and replacing Saddam's regime with a more benign leadership.[4]

It could be argued, however, that successful attainment of the regime change goal undermined rather than advanced the U.S. interest of national security. While we achieved our goal of toppling the regime, this victory produced the unintended consequence of an unraveling of the Iraqi state apparatus and a slide towards civil war. What had been a strong state quickly turned into a struggling, fragile state—an outcome with the potential to undermine U.S. national security interests. The resulting chaos and instability facilitated the creation of a fresh base from which al-Qaeda could wage battle against the United States. While it is true that later strategies, such as the surge of 2006 and the Sunni Awakening, were effective in rolling back the threat from al-Qaeda in Iraq, it is still not clear that this produced anything other than tactical advantages for the United States. It was the fact that achievement of the goals undermined core national security interests of the United States that accounts for this.

WHAT IS THE DIFFERENCE BETWEEN A GOAL AND A STRATEGY?

One might think that differentiating between goals and strategies should be easy and straightforward. Goals are the desired end-state, while the strategy involves the methods or ways for achieving that end-state goal. Goals are what need to be accomplished, and strategy involves how they are to be accomplished. But this clear distinction notwithstanding, differentiating goals from strategies can sometimes be confusing. Was containment of the Soviet Union during the Cold War a goal or a strategy?[5] Without knowing the intent of policymakers at the time, one could be excused for thinking that containing Soviet expansionism was in fact the end-state goal. But in reality, the architects of containment saw it not as the desired end-state, but rather as a mechanism that would ultimately lead to internal turmoil, economic decay, and the eventual collapse of the Soviet Union. To them, containment of the Soviet Union was not a goal, but rather a strategy.[6]

With that in mind, the practitioner needs to make sure that the stated goal is actually the desired end-state. If what sounds like and even appears to be a goal is actually an intermediate point toward, or catalyst of, another desired end-state, like in the previous example of Soviet containment, then it is more than likely a strategy. When thinking about this distinction between goals and strategies within the context of different levels of a government or business, things can get even trickier. This is because the goal set at a lower level can actually be part of a strategy at a higher level. It may be that selling a certain number of Kindle e-readers is a goal for the sales department of Amazon. But at Amazon's corporate level, the launch of e-readers into the market is actually part of a strategy that serves the goal of capturing a larger share of the book business market. So, the goal of the sales department may actually be a corporate strategy. What this should illustrate is that when dealing with different levels of an organization, there is nothing contradictory about the achievement of a goal at a lower level being part of a strategy at a higher level. The problem comes when, as in the illustration of containment, a strategy is mistaken for a goal at the highest level of an organization or government.

THE CRITERIA FOR GOALS: SETTING METRICS

Although strategists may not always tell the outside world how success of a particular strategy will be measured, they need to be clear with themselves and their teams what benchmarks will be used. With vague and ambiguous goals, it may be impossible to know when, or if, success has been achieved. Therefore, to the degree possible, goals should be stated in clear and unambiguous terms. This should not be interpreted to mean that all strategic goals need to be expressed in quantitative terms; but it does mean that the goal should be sufficiently clear so as to point to either success or failure of the strategy.

For illustration purposes, let's look at a case where strategic goals are stated in obscure, rather than clear, terms. One example would be a U.S.-based computer company with a goal to successfully enter the Chinese market. While the statement expresses a clear statement of intent, it does not represent a clearly stated goal. There are several critical omissions that make it unclear. First, it is difficult to know when the goal has been met. Is it when the company secures its first small customer in China? Or when the company reaches $500 million in sales revenue? Based on how the goal is stated, these questions are unanswerable. Moreover, no timeframe is specified. If the company achieves market entry in five years, will it have fulfilled its goal? Or is the expectation that market entry will take place within the first year? The goal is almost meaningless, as none of these critical benchmarks are set.

There are several possible ways to fortify the goal of the U.S. computer company. One way is to anchor it to something that can be tracked over a specified period of time. For example, they could set a specific sales volume and profitability level. The goal could be to generate $25 million of annual revenue and $1 million in annual profits in the Chinese market by 2013. Or another clear goal could be to achieve the number-three rank in China's market share within three years. By stating the goals this way, it will be clear at any point in time how the company is tracking relative to its expected performance.

On the foreign policy side, the issue of making clear goals is a bit more complex. In the foreign policy milieu, goals flow from interests, but also from the policy considerations that mediate those interests.[7] Because of the realities of operating in such complex political environments, policymakers may try to give themselves political maneuverability and flexibility by keeping goals intentionally ambiguous. They could do this for a couple of different reasons. The first is that very specific goals can box policymakers in and set them up for failure, since goals that aren't met can become fodder for opponents and detractors. Sometimes goals are kept nebulous in order to make consensus building easier among parties not naturally predisposed towards agreement. Ambiguously stated goals can also give policymakers the flexibility to adjust once safely outside the spotlight of public debate.[8] As a case in point, Bob Woodward, in his book *Obama's Wars*, chronicles the debate that erupted over whether to state goals for the war in Afghanistan in explicit or vague terms. Secretary of Defense Robert Gates wanted the goal stated in uncharacteristically specific terms—to defeat the Taliban—but had opposition from some in the National Security Council who thought that a vaguer goal of "disrupting" the Taliban would give the administration greater room to maneuver.[9]

TYPES OF GOALS: PRIMARY VS. SUBSIDIARY GOALS

Aside from the political considerations referred to previously, there are times when it is desirable to make goals clear but keep them as general as possible. One purpose of creating a high-level, general goal is to provide strategic focus on a singular, overarching objective, which encompasses the entire organization and its primary strategic initiative. We can call this high-level goal the primary goal. In 2010, for example, a primary goal of the United States' National Security Strategy was to make Iraq "sovereign, stable and self-reliant."[10] What this goal lacked in measurability was made up for by the simple way it explains the overarching mission in Iraq to the U.S. government departments, as well as to Iraqi and U.S. citizens.

But as invaluable as this primary goal is, it needs to be supplemented with far more granular goals. This is where subsidiary goals come into play. Whereas primary goals can be thought of as the highest level for a particular strategy, subsidiary goals are more specific expressions of, and derived from, primary goals. Subsidiary goals are more measurable and specific, while primary goals may be broader and more sweeping.[11]

The key is that achieving subsidiary goals advances the attainment of the primary goal. So how could the sweeping primary goal to make Iraq sovereign, stable, and self-reliant be translated into more granular goals for the U.S. Department of Defense and the U.S. Department of State? One subsidiary goal might be to reduce the number of insurgency attacks on Iraqi military and civilian targets by 75 percent within one year. Other subsidiary goals might be to hold national elections and have a specified number of Iraqi soldiers trained and armed by a certain date. Notice that these time-bound subsidiary goals roll up to and support the more general primary goal. Now we have a general goal that captures the overarching strategic objective, and several subsidiary goals against which success can be measured.

Let's look at the distinction between primary and subsidiary goals within a business context. A company like Dell Computer would set a primary goal of improving customer service. This goal is clear, yet difficult to measure without being made more specific. To make this goal more meaningful, the company would create subsidiary goals that were managed by a number of different departments within the business. For example, the customer service department would need to set specific metrics, such as the maximum lead times for shipping a product after receiving an order from a customer, as well as guidelines for acceptable hold-times on inbound tech support phone calls.[12] The production, sales, and marketing departments would also come up with their own very specific subsidiary goals that would be subsumed by the primary goal of improving customer service.

One could reasonably argue that the notion of primary goals corresponds to what is commonly referred to as grand strategy goals in a government milieu, or corporate strategy goals in business, while subsidiary goals correspond to goals set at lower levels, such as a government's national security strategy goals or a company's marketing strategy goals. One could also reasonably argue that primary goals exist at what is commonly thought of as the strategic level, while subsidiary goals exist at what we refer to as the operational or tactical levels. I have avoided this nomenclature for several reasons. The first is that the distinctions between different levels of strategy can be culturally specific rather than universally applicable. The second is that there is a trap in viewing strategy as residing only at the highest level of an organization, with operations and tactics taking place at lower levels. While in some organizations this may actually be the case, this type of thinking is not particularly useful for organizations trying to encourage or impart strategic thinking across all levels. The distinction between primary and subsidiary goals is a more neutral and generally applicable way to think about this concept.

TYPES OF GOALS: MILESTONE GOALS

As has been discussed previously, making sure that goals are measurable is absolutely critical in determining the success or failure of a particular strategy. But in addition to measuring success or failure, the strategist needs to be able to track intermediate progress toward a goal. This is particularly important for goals that are cast far into the future, where the strategist can't afford to wait until the end to measure progress. The notion of milestone goals can be particularly useful in helping the strategist bridge the gap between long-term goals and the need to measure progress in the short to medium term.

Milestones are markers that show progress along the road toward the fulfillment of a goal. While it might appear that setting milestone goals is easy, it is tougher than one might imagine. If progress toward goals always proceeded in an even and linear fashion, it would be easy to set these intermediate markers. Progress towards the goal would continue at a steady pace, with the strategist needing only to decide the time intervals at which to measure results. For example if a business's goal is to generate $1 million of annual sales revenue within five years, and management wanted to set milestone goals at one year intervals, then a linear projection would show $200,000 of revenue in year one, $400,000 in year two, $600,000 in year three, $800,000 in year four, and finally $1 million in the fifth year.

But strategies seldom deliver linear traction toward goals. Setting milestone goals, therefore, is far more complicated. Depending on how quickly the strategy is designed to develop traction, progress measured in milestone goals is sometimes front-loaded and sometimes back-loaded. Front-loaded goals are set when a quick success is expected in the beginning, with traction losing momentum over time. In this kind of situation, a company that was projecting $1 million of annual sales revenue within five years might set a milestone goal of $400,000 in sales for year one, $600,000 year two, $800,000 in year three, $900,000 in year four, and $1 million of sales in year five. Notice that traction is expected early, with progress slowing over time.

Back-loaded goals work in the opposite direction. In these kinds of situations progress will be slower in the early years, with the traction picking up as time marches on. Let's assume that the primary goal for the U.S. military in Afghanistan is to reverse what the Taliban has gained over the past few years.[13] In order to develop milestone goals, we first need at least one measurable goal. Since the primary goal is not measurable, let's work with a more precise subsidiary goal, which hypothetically could be to wrest thirty villages from the clutches of the Taliban in several different provinces within two years. One would expect that little progress would be made in the first year. Milestone goals set at six-month intervals might show that in the first six months, three villages are projected to be secured, with four more by the end of the first year. But in the second year, ten villages are projected to be secured in the first six months, with the last thirteen being secured in the second six month period. Traction is expected to build momentum over time, so milestone goals would be set according to the expected pace of traction.

How does the strategist know whether to set milestone goals showing even, front-loaded, or back-loaded progress? This will be determined by assumptions the strategist makes about the nature of the competition, and what obstacles or start-up issues are expected. Setting milestone goals for a company's sales revenue for a new product over a five year period would require taking into account expectations of customer receptivity to the new product and any competition that might ensue. Assumptions about how quickly a given strategy can be rolled out, launched, and made operational also would need to be factored in, as would how quickly the company can marshal its resources and ramp up its capabilities. Depending on these factors, the company may decide that sales of the new product may start at a slow pace for the first two years, but then pick up starting in the third year. Sales may be constrained in the early years because of competitive pressures, slow customer acceptance to the new product, or start-up manufacturing problems. So milestone goals in this case would be back-loaded.

What factors might suggest that milestone goals should be front-loaded? Assume a company introduces a brand-new product, with competition expected to appear only after the first year. Moreover, focus groups indicate that customer receptivity will be strong right out of the blocks. In this case, the company might expect an early spike in sales but a loss of momentum over time. The assumption is that competition will eventually catch up and make the early growth rate unsustainable, thus the front-loaded milestone goals.

TYPES OF GOALS: STATUS QUO VS. SURGE GOALS

There are more substantive distinctions among goals that need to be made as well. It is important to distinguish goals based on what the strategist's objectives and ambitions are relative to the external environment. We will look at two general types of goals in this regard—the status quo goals, which aim to preserve and contain, and surge goals, which aim to disrupt and upend.

Status Quo Goals: Preservation

The desired end-state of status quo goals is preservation of what already exists. Containing the advance of a military opponent is an example of a status quo military goal, while preserving stability in a region or country is a status quo political goal. A type of status quo corporate goal would be to protect a company's current high market share.[14] Notice that these types of goals don't alter the strategic environment; rather, they protect it.

There are a number of illustrative examples to choose from to highlight status quo goals. What follows are a few more examples from different sectors:

1. U.S. military goal: to deny al-Qaeda a safe haven in Afghanistan.[15] Since the presumption is that al-Qaeda currently has no base in Afghanistan, the idea is to deny them something they currently don't have and preserve a situation that exists.

2. Computer company goal: to maintain market share of 25 percent over the next two years. In this case, the idea is that the company doesn't necessarily need to grow its market share, just preserve the share it has.

3. Israeli foreign policy goal: to prevent al-Qaeda from establishing a base in the Gaza Strip. Again, the presumption is that the status quo is being preserved since al-Qaeda doesn't currently have a base in Gaza.

Surge Goals: Disruption

In contrast to status quo goals, the desired end-state of surge goals is to alter the landscape in some significant way.[16] Rather than protect the status quo, surge goals involve shaping or disrupting the strategic environment. Saddam Hussein's goal to seize Kuwait in 1990 and the U.S. military's goal to roll the Iraqi military back from Kuwait in 1991 would both be examples of a surge goal.

Strategists planning surge goals need to understand the assumptions they are making, and the potential implications. In some cases surge goals may be viable only because the political, military, or business environment is already at a precipice of change and disrupting the status quo is possible because it has already become unstable. One could argue that the Egyptian protesters' goal of deposing President Hosni Mubarak in 2011 was based on the assumption that the earlier overthrow of Tunisia's president, Zine el-Abidine Ben Ali, made the social and political environment in their own country ripe for change. Another assumption might be that while the environment may not be ready for change, there is sufficient capability and resources to overcome the barriers that prevent it. In other words, the goal may be viable given the capability of the strategist to actually produce and control the change that is the desired end-state

What follows are some further examples of surge goals:

1. U.S. military goals for Afghanistan: one of the goals the U.S. has set in Afghanistan is to reverse the Taliban's momentum and deny it the ability to overthrow the Afghan government. Notice that the emphasis here is focused on rolling back positions held by the opponent. Another goal is to strengthen the capacity of the Afghan security forces and government so that they can take lead responsibility for Afghanistan's future.[17] This is a surge goal, because it involves strengthening an ally so as to be able to take on the Taliban. But at another level, it is also a status quo goal, since it also helps preserve the position of the Afghan government.

2. U.S. diplomatic goal for Iran: to persuade Iran to renounce its uranium enrichment program.[18] This is an example of a surge goal, as it involves rolling back an initiative the opponent had already commenced.

Why call these surge and status quo goals rather than use the more familiar nomenclature of offensive and defensive goals? There is nothing intrinsically wrong with referring to goals as either offensive or defensive, other than the fact that it can be very limiting and lead to rigidity in strategic thinking. The offensive/defensive dichotomy represents a useful way to describe one's overall position vis-à-vis an opponent. It can be a useful way to delineate the type of strategy and strategic methods used in a competitive situation, but it gets trickier when trying to extend this terminology to goals. The defensive vs. offensive dichotomy is most useful when describing one's competitive position relative to achieving a goal, and less useful when describing the goal itself. Moreover, one's position in a maneuver can fluctuate from defensive to offensive many times over the course of a campaign, while goals as desired end-states generally remain more fixed. Using the terms "surge" and "status quo" help us distinguish between one's strategic position vis-à-vis the opponent and one's goals relative to that opponent.

One question the strategist might ponder is whether surge and status quo goals are mutually exclusive? In other words, can an organization combine both types of goals in a single strategic situation? The answer is generally yes. It is not unusual for a business or a government to have surge as well as status quo goals in the same campaign. Take some of the goals that are presented in the U.S. Defense Department Quadrennial Defense Review 2010, for example.

The Defense Review comprises both surge and status quo (what the U.S. military calls steady-state) goals for the United States involvement in Afghanistan. One of the surge goals is to reverse the momentum of the Taliban. The goal is to change the status quo by disrupting the momentum that has been created by the insurgency. But in tandem with that is a status quo goal of denying the Taliban access to and control of key population and production centers and lines of communication.[19] Why are these not inconsistent? One involves reversing the Taliban's position, while the other involves containing the Taliban's position relative to key population centers. They are consistent because the surge goal is at a different level than the status quo goal. The surge goal is a primary goal, which involves turning the tide of the battle away from the Taliban and toward the United States, its allies, and the Afghan government. It is designed to change the overall dynamic of the strategic situation. The status quo goal of preserving control of territory and population centers already held is a short-term subsidiary goal that supports the higher-level and longer-term primary goal of turning the tide away from the Taliban. While cast at different levels and different time frames, they in fact are complementary.

CONCLUSION

As we have seen, goal setting is a complicated and challenging part of the strategy process, and it is anything but prosaic. Setting goals should never be conducted in a vacuum but rather should be set within the context of an organization's interests and capabilities. The strategist should be familiar with the different types of goals. Using subsidiary and primary goals helps the strategist set desired end-states at different levels, and milestone goals help the strategist set benchmarks for tracking progress over time. The strategist should also be clear about the assumptions they are making when they set either status quo or surge goals.

2 THE PRIMACY OF CAPABILITY

With strategy there is always a struggle to keep an eye on the forest without losing sight of the trees. This is particularly true when looking at strategy through an inward lens onto an organization, business, or country. While it is tempting to focus attention on an organization's (or country's) resources, it is critical that strategists pay primary attention to channeling these resources into strategic capability. Capability should be thought of as the muscle of strategy, and "manufacturing" it involves more than merely identifying and allocating resources.[1]

What this means is that manufacturing capability out of resources is not ancillary, but rather an essential part of the strategy-making process. To the degree that strategy is about closing the gap between large goals and proportionately smaller resources, capability is the bridge to do this. Another way to think about it is that transforming inert resources into more muscular capability contributes to the multiplier effect that is so important in any strategic undertaking.[2]

The understanding that creating capability is a high-level strategic function, while managing resources is more operational, is a hallmark of a strategic organization. First-rate companies understand that their strategic focus needs to be more on capabilities, called core competencies, than on the resources that fuel them.[3] The focus on capabilities has also become the preoccupation of military strategists. MacKubin Thomas Owens from the Naval War College makes the point eloquently by arguing that "resources are not means until strategy provides some understanding of how they will be organized and employed."[4] This doesn't imply that resources aren't critically important, only that they are insufficient for strategy. In order to enable a strategy, resources have to be configured, combined, managed, and converted into a more muscular capability.

THE PRIMACY OF CAPABILITY OVER RESOURCES

It would not be overstating the point to say that preparing a country or organization for a strategy by marshalling its capability is one of the most important functions a strategist will perform. Unless the strategist has thoroughly thought through which capabilities are necessary to power a given strategy, the availability of large amounts of resources won't necessarily redound to the benefit of a business or country. Thinking through how these resources get channeled into capability is the prime task for the strategist, and the major determinant of whether a strategy can be properly executed.

One question that needs to be addressed is, how can we conceptually distinguish between capabilities and resources? Think of capability as the organizational equivalent of a finely tuned muscle that makes a range of motion and action possible—like a muscle, the capabilities of an organization or country give it the potential to act, even when not fully flexed. Capability is the set of strengths that powers an organization's strategy and prepares it for action.

If capability can be thought of as the muscle of strategy, resources can be thought of as the nutrients that feed and enable that muscle. In contrast to the kinetic, muscular nature of capability, resources are inert. Until integrated, organized, and leveraged on behalf of creating capability, resources lack energy and potential.

Let's look at a couple of examples to further highlight the distinction between capabilities and resources. Apple's core capabilities can be identified as design, innovation, and marketing. These are the main capabilities that distinguish the company and animate its strategies. Notice that these are intangible qualities—strengths that are bigger than just a compilation of tangible resources. Each of these capabilities requires a set of resources. The design and innovation capabilities require equipment, engineers, designers, and an organizational structure that reinforces excellence. The marketing capability is supported by computer technologies as well as financial and human capital resources. But, while the resources are necessary, the company is mainly focused on managing the resources, as well as the processes and culture of the business, to create the design, innovation, and marketing capabilities.

Moving to a national security context, the United States could be said to have a retaliatory strike military capability. This means that it has the ability to punish any aggressor and respond with a second strike. But this intangible retaliatory capability is not just a function of the resources the military has at its disposal. An integration of effort, planning, and leadership are all needed to transform these inert resources into a muscular strategic capability.

How can a focus on capability help one think strategically? The resources available to an organization or country may be relatively fixed. For example, a company has finite financial and capital resources, and a country has limits in terms of men, material, and natural resources. The strategist, whose gaze remains on these fixed resources rather than at the higher-level capability, is likely to think about strategy in very unimaginative and linear terms. He or she is likely to set goals that are proportionate to available resources. In contrast, the consummate strategist thinks about innovative ways for deploying those finite resources such that a much larger and expansive set of capabilities are imagined. He or she will understand that the potential to generate capability may be elastic and expansive, even under conditions of resource constraints. Strategists who focus at the level of capability are likely to think imaginatively about how to use scarce resources to achieve outsized goals.

Here is an example of a case where relatively limited resources get used creatively to generate a much larger and robust set of capabilities. The terrorist organization, al-Qaeda, was clearly imaginative in thinking about how to create a multiplier effect on its resources. They developed a way to deploy a fixed, relatively finite supply of resources in order to create a much more expansive supply of capability. Al-Qaeda's tangible resources involved box cutters, relatively small financial assets, and the apparently expendable lives of the suicide hijackers. Through the more intangible capabilities of imagination, coordination, and planning, the hijackers were able to exact a toll on the United States disproportionate to the paltry resources they had at their disposal.[5] Had al-Qaeda focused only on the financial, manpower, and weaponry resources they had available to them, it is unlikely they would have ever considered challenging a superpower like the United States. Instead, they raised their sights and conceptualized how these resources could yield a powerful asymmetric fighting capability through training, planning, and coordination.

While French general André Beaufre predated the emergence of al-Qaeda, his comments on strategy are nonetheless relevant. He argued that strategy "is not like chess; its pieces have no permanent, defined value. It must therefore produce its solutions by a sort of cookery, fusing together constantly changing ingredients."[6] This suitably describes al-Qaeda, who cobbled together meager resources to manufacture extraordinary capability in order to achieve outsized goals. It is also germane to any organization whose strategic focus is on capabilities as well as on resources.

So where should the strategist start when thinking about generating capability within an organization? There are several questions that should be asked. The first is what is the country or business capable of at the present? The next question is whether or not the current capabilities are sufficient to meet the goals of the strategy being considered? Are they sufficient, or do new capabilities need to be generated? This analysis requires a hard-nosed assessment of the portfolio of capabilities required for the strategic challenges at hand, as well as an analysis of the gap between current capabilities and what is necessary to go forward.[7]

CAPABILITY GAP ANALYSIS

The first step in a strategic capability analysis is to identify the gaps. The U.S. Quadrennial Defense Review Report (QDR) of 2006 is an example of a capability gap analysis. The focus of the QDR is on the military capabilities and the resources needed to deal with the strategic challenges facing the United States at that time. The 2006 version of this document is particularly illustrative of how the Defense Department identified, and planned to close, the gaps it saw between the existing military capabilities and the capabilities required for challenges in the future.

The QDR authors clearly believed that the United States had a robust set of capabilities for dealing with strategic challenges from conventional nation-states, but was lacking in capabilities for contending with threats from violent non-state actors like al-Qaeda. The United States had developed its existing portfolio of capabilities during the Cold War, when it faced off against an adversary, the Soviet Union and its allies, whose capabilities were symmetric and similar to our own. But after the Cold War the nature of the challenges facing the United States changed dramatically. In addition to facing affronts from traditional nation states, the United States was forced to contend with new non-state adversaries like al-Qaeda, which possessed dissimilar, asymmetric capabilities.

This assessment rested on assumptions about the nature of the new opponent. In contrast to a more lumbering superpower like the Soviet Union, al-Qaeda was an agile, flexible adversary. To effectively combat this new kind of enemy, U.S. fighting forces need to be more quick-footed and responsive—attributes that would only be possible with a new set of capabilities.

One gap the QDR drafters identified was between the discrete capabilities of the military services currently in place and the more integrated joint capability required to confront unconventional threats. They determined that while traditional strategic challenges were served well by a division of labor between the different military services and between military and civilian departments, contending with non-traditional opponents required greater interagency cooperation between the different branches of government.

Traditionally the army, navy, air force, and marines have each had their own set of capabilities and responses to national security threats and each tends to operate relatively autonomously. This "stove-piped" system worked well when the United States faced off against adversaries organized according to a similar division of labor. But this is inadequate for meeting the challenges from asymmetric threats, like al-Qaeda or weak or fragile states. The QDR authors argued that more cooperation and integration across the different military services in the form of a joint force capability was required to fill the gap between the existing and required capabilities.[8] This new joint force capability would be seamless, with each of the military services acting in tandem against threats. It would require different command and control structures, organizational reform, and improved communication between the different arms of the U.S. military.

Another gap identified was between the "one-size-fits-all deterrence" capability established during the Cold War and the type of deterrence capability required against more unconventional threats. While a one-size-fits-all deterrent capability was adequate for a bipolar world, the emergence of a much messier international system requires a more customized approach. Whereas a nuclear deterrent was appropriate for dissuading great powers from aggression, other types of deterrence are needed to contend with challenges from other nation-states as well as non-state actors like al-Qaeda. According to the QDR, a tailored deterrence capability is necessary to fill this gap.[9] This deterrence would be powered by nuclear assets, as well as conventional military assets, and has the capacity to build deterrence on the fly for new emerging threats.

Joint force and tailored deterrence were just two of the many necessary capabilities the 2006 QDR identified to fill the gap between the existing portfolio of capabilities and the capabilities the United States requires for confronting future national security threats. The document also specified the particular resources that would be needed to power these capabilities. It identified which armaments and equipment needed to be phased out and which needed to be phased in. It also discussed the kind of rebalancing of human and tangible assets that would be necessary to support the new capabilities. But the important takeaway is that the focus of the document was more on capabilities, and less on resources. The resources were treated as ingredients for capabilities, important but only to the degree that they helped the military close the gap between present and needed capabilities.

Businesses also go through the wrenching process of reengineering their capabilities to fill gaps in order to meet changing realities. Flagging financial or sales performance often becomes the impetus for creating a new portfolio of capabilities. Sometimes it is the arrival of a new CEO with a different strategic vision for the company. While there are numerous examples of companies which have had to reengineer their capabilities, the case of the Gillette Company's transformation prior to its acquisition by Proctor and Gamble (P&G) in 2005 is particularly illustrative.

Jim Kilts was brought to the Gillette Company in 2001 as CEO to reverse the company's lackluster financial performance. In order to turn the company's situation around, the energetic and dynamic Kilts was determined to push the business in new strategic directions. He wanted to make sure that the company had a "good," "better," and "best" alternative for customers in each of its many product lines. He also thought it necessary to rationalize the numerous individual brands, like Braun, Duracell, and Gillette, that fell under the company's umbrella brand. In addition, he planned to assess the financial contribution of each of the different divisions of the company. In order to accomplish these new strategic initiatives, he identified several gaps in the company's existing capability portfolio, and set on a path for filling each of them.

One of these new capabilities was something he called a financial performance capability. While the company's old financial capability had involved reporting past results, there was little capacity for helping the executive team manage and guide the company toward future financial performance. What Kilts needed was a financial capability that was more forward-leaning and integrated into the business decision making process.

He envisioned a new financial management capability in which the newly constituted financial team would work closely with each of the business units to enhance their financial performance. Creating this required Kilts to force a massive reorganization of the financial departments of the company. The result was a capability that allowed the company's financial team to analyze trends and data from each of the business units, and then use that data proactively to help manage the various businesses. Moreover, the financial team also worked with the business unit managers who were developing key strategic initiatives to make sure they were financially sound and sustainable.[10] In other words, the new capability used analysis, not just to report on the past, but also to help manage the company and its constituent business units for future success. Creating this new financial capability was instrumental in Kilts's turnaround of Gillette, his ability to execute his new strategies, and in his positioning of the company for its eventual acquisition by P&G for $57 billion. Kilts's comprehension of the gap between the company's existing capabilities and what was required for the future was instrumental to his repositioning strategy for the company.

LINCHPIN CAPABILITIES

Typically a strategy requires not one but a repertoire of capabilities. In order to be effective, an organization needs to make sure that its strategic capabilities complement one another, are internally consistent, and mutually reinforcing. The key is to make sure that the different capabilities work together as a system. So, in addition to analyzing any capability gaps that may exist, it is important to understand how the various capabilities of an organization or government relate to one another. Part of this involves the strategist determining whether the various capabilities in his or her organization's portfolio are equally critical for strategic success, or whether some capabilities have primacy over others. In addition, the strategist also needs to determine whether the different capabilities function independently of one another, or whether some capabilities are dependent on the effectiveness of others.

This notion of some capabilities being dependent on the effectiveness of others is important for strategists analyzing their own organizations, or analyzing the capabilities of their adversaries. Is there one or more capabilities upon which the effectiveness of other capabilities hinges, serving as a sort of linchpin? Or do all of the capabilities more or less operate independently of one another? A linchpin capability exists if, in its absence, other strategic capabilities are rendered ineffective. Figuring out the linchpin capability is important for strategists, as it points to what the priorities should be in terms of resource allocation. The most instrumental capabilities will probably need the greatest resources. It also is important in understanding which capabilities need to be the most fortified and protected. While all capabilities of an organization may be important, it will be absolutely critical to ensure that the linchpin capability is in place and shielded.[11] Linchpin capabilities are the most important capability for executing a given strategy, but they can also be an Achilles' heel or convenient, high yield target for an opponent.

Which capability serves as the linchpin can shift along with changes in the nature of the strategic challenge or opportunity—they are not hard-wired but instead are organized and configured around particular challenges. The capabilities the United States needs to combat al-Qaeda are a good illustration of linchpin capabilities, and how they get organized around specific challenges. Among others, the primary capabilities the United States needs are an enhanced intelligence capability, a partnership alliance capability, and an integrated joint-force capability.[12] The United States needs the ability to track and monitor al-Qaeda operatives and financial transactions, forge strong allies across the globe to assist in counterterrorism challenges, and integrate efforts across the different military services.

All of these capabilities are important to effectively confront a challenge from an opponent like al-Qaeda, but is there one that serves as the linchpin upon which all others depend? Arguably the single most important capability is the partnership-alliance capability. Al-Qaeda is a global terror organization with a footprint that spans many countries. Confronting it, therefore, requires partners across the globe with whom the United States can coordinate its counterterrorism efforts. Unless the capability to work with European as well as Middle Eastern, Asian, and African allies is in place, the capabilities of enhanced intelligence and joint-forces will be rendered less effective. In other words, in the absence of robust, global partnerships and alliances, the intelligence capability won't translate into a competitive advantage against al-Qaeda. Similarly, joint-forces integration is a critical capability, provided it can be linked to the efforts of regional alliance partners. Without these partnerships the integration of effort across the different military services will have limited effectiveness.

The notion of a linchpin capability also applies in a business milieu; take, for example, the Walt Disney Company. The capabilities that enabled its strategy were set building, costume design, brand management, customer service, and storytelling.[13] Among these, which of any is the linchpin for Disney? One could argue that storytelling is the linchpin. Without Disney's ability to spin a tale using its legendary and beloved characters, the set building, brand management, and costume design capabilities will be rendered irrelevant. Unless the company is able to continuously create compelling content, the other capabilities are strategically meaningless.

Figuring out the relationships among the different capabilities of an organization should be thought of as a key part of strategy making. This is as much a part of strategy as is battling a business competitor in the marketplace, or challenging an opponent on the political or military battlefield. It requires building a system of capabilities that are integrated, and figuring out how different capabilities relate to one another, and which one is the linchpin. While all of these concepts are part of the inward face of strategy, they are critical to launching outwardly directed strategies against an opponent.

CHANNELING RESOURCES INTO CAPABILITY

As mentioned, it is easy to lose sight of capability if one has his or her eye mostly on resources. But there is also a danger in the other direction. While it is critical to keep one's gaze on capabilities, this should not come at the expense of an awareness of the resources necessary to power those capabilities. It is important to balance a focus on capability with an understanding of what resources an organization has available, and it is critical to understand how an organization uses its resources to create capability.

There are several ways resources can be used by a country or organization. Resources can be deployed, held in reserve for later deployment as "dry powder," or used for bargaining purposes. Sometimes the same resources can serve more than one of these purposes. But in order for the reader to grasp the different ways resources can be used, each one will be treated separately.

Deployed Resources

As the fuel of strategic capability, some resources will be used as the strategy is executed. How they get deployed will vary by the specifics of the strategic circumstances, but a combination of financial, human, and hardware assets will be deployed to launch and then sustain almost any type of business or military strategy.

Resources targeted for deployment can be either expendable or fixed. Expendable assets are consumed and drawn down in the execution of strategy. Like the fuel in a car, expendable resources need to be replaced or renewed as the operation continues. Examples of expendable resources for a business are financial assets and raw material inventory, which gets spent or drawn down as the course of a strategy unfolds. For a military, expendable assets are weaponry and munitions. While not all weaponry and munitions get consumed in battle, there will be a rate at which they are used or destroyed and must be replaced. The strategist needs to project the rate of depletion of these resources in a given strategic situation.

Fixed resources are resources that are deployed in the implementation of the strategy but don't necessarily get consumed. Oftentimes these fixed assets are part of the infrastructure of the organization itself. For a company these might be manufacturing facilities and equipment, which may be adapted and even enlarged on behalf of a new strategy but are largely fixed and don't get consumed as strategy marches on. For a military, fixed assets will be bases of operations, certain types of aircraft, and ships. They get deployed in battle, but usually don't get drawn down or depleted.

"Dry Powder" Resources

There are some resources that almost any organization will want to hold in reserve to ensure that a given capability can be sustained over time, or to use for any future crisis contingency. These can be called "dry powder" assets, meaning they are kept out of commission for possible use in the future. These dry powder assets could merely be the surplus of a deployable asset. In financial investment strategies you often see part of the asset portfolio get invested, while the other part is held on the sidelines in cash as dry powder for later deployment.

But sometimes dry powder resources are a completely different type than those that are being deployed. Some companies may decide to hold a new product on the sidelines, delaying its introduction until market and competitive conditions improve.[14] Technology companies are also known to do this. They sometimes withhold certain technological innovations from the market, allowing the competition to reveal its hand first. If the company believes it has a superior product, it may want the competition to move first, and then trump it later with its better product. They hold new products or product innovations on the sidelines as dry powder for deployment at a more strategically opportune moment.

Bargaining Resources

Some resources are never intended for deployment but are acquired in order to create bargaining leverage. While resources accumulated primarily for bargaining purposes could be deployed in theory, the risks and costs associated with actual deployment often far outweigh any possible benefit. Nuclear weaponry is the paradigmatic example of such a resource. Most countries acquire nuclear weapons, less with an intent to use them, but more to restrain the behavior of adversaries and to yield bargaining strength in any negotiation. And, while a rogue state or violent non-state actor could acquire a nuclear device with the express purpose of using it, that is more the exception than the norm.

Businesses, too, use some assets for bargaining purposes only. Financial capital, for example, can be used as a bargaining asset. A company may signal that it is willing to use its superior financial balance sheet to wage a price war, should there be any attempts by an aggressive, or smaller and less financially powerful, competitor to try to steal customers and market share through predatory pricing. The idea is that a company's deep financial pockets, along with either an explicit or implicit threat to retaliate with a protracted price war, would have a deterrent effect on a competitor considering lowering its prices. The smaller or weaker company knows that the larger company with deep pockets can sustain a long and bloody price war, while it cannot. Thus having the financial asset capacity to wage a price war can be used as a bargaining chip.

CONCLUSION

Capability serves as the muscle of strategy. The manufacturing of capability is one of the main strategic functions that constitute the inward face of strategy. It is through the conversion of mostly inert, finite resources into more expansive, muscular capability that the multiplier effect of strategy gets created. For this reason, the strategist from almost any type of organization will need to focus attention on the capabilities required to make a particular strategy possible. This involves taking inventory of the organization's current capabilities, and then comparing this to the requirements of the strategic challenges at hand. This type of analysis will indicate the gaps between current and future capabilities that need to be filled. The strategist also needs to understand how different capabilities relate to one another. While an organization may need a wide range of capabilities, there may be a linchpin capability that has primacy. Linchpin capabilities are the most critical capability in a given strategy, without which other capabilities are rendered ineffective.

But as much as they are a source of strength, the fact that so much of the overall capability is concentrated at this point also makes linchpin capabilities a point of incredible vulnerability. In addition, the strategist also needs to understand the different way resources get managed on behalf of creating capabilities.

PART 2

THE OUTWARD FACE OF STRATEGY

3 STRATEGY IN THE DIMENSION OF SYSTEMS

N
ow that the inward face of strategy has been addressed, it is important to consider how the success of strategies is determined by how well the strategist navigates the treacherous waters of the external environment. We will start by looking at the outward face of strategy within the dimension of systems.

Systems are all around us and greatly impact our lives, yet we have a tendency to pay them little heed. One reason for this is that focusing on systems involves some level of abstraction. It is much easier to ponder how tangible, immediate threats and opportunities affect our lives than it is to think about the impact of something as intangible as a system. Consider how we tend to think about the Arab Spring that erupted in 2011. A natural tendency is to look for the immediate causes of revolt in individual countries like Tunisia, Egypt, Libya, Syria, and Yemen. But we are less likely to address the higher-level questions about the dynamics in the Middle East regional system that contributed to the spread of eruptions across the Arab world, and how these regional dynamics affect U.S. interests. The same syndrome occurs in the business world. Business executives ponder daily how to battle the immediate and tangible challenges from their competitors, but tend to give only passing thought to how the structure of the industry system their companies operate within defines, shapes, and influences their competitiveness and potential for profitability. In both foreign policy and business, the most proximate, immediate, and tangible threats get the most attention, while the broader and more abstract systemic effects get short shrift.

The strategist, however, cannot afford to ignore systems. Even though it requires stretching to a certain level of abstraction, understanding and manipulating systems of behavior is an incredibly important part of strategy for a couple of reasons. It sensitizes the strategist to the fact that competition between two opponents doesn't take place in a vacuum, but rather within a systemic context. A systems approach to strategy doesn't ignore the opponent, but rather looks at competition within a much broader context. It is vital that the strategist understand the context within which competition takes place, thus strategy in the dimension of system aims to adapt to or shape the environmental context in order to improve one's competitive advantage.

Understanding systems is also important because it could very well be the secret sauce of a strategy. Since one's opponent may not be thinking and operating at this high level, competitive advantage can be created by taking systems into account when planning a strategy. Moreover, advantages accrue from the fact that strategy in the dimension of systems might escape detection by the opponent, as these strategies don't confront the opponent directly. Instead, they work by trying to influence the external environment, and are less likely to appear on the opponent's threat radar screen.

Lastly, thinking in system terms is important because it widens one's strategic horizon, opening up the possibility for new options to triumph over an opponent. It will force creative thinking and raise one's sights to think about indirect ways to influence the behavior of the opponent.

Before going any further it is critical to understand how thinking and acting in the systems dimension can improve one's competitive strategy game. Strategy at its very heart involves getting others to do what they might not otherwise do.[1] This may involve getting an adversarial country's government to bend to your country's will, or it may involve persuading consumers to buy your product instead of the competition's. Convincing or compelling others to do something they aren't naturally inclined to do involves the creation and exploitation of leverage. In other words, it takes a certain amount of bargaining power or leverage to get an enemy country to accede to your position, and it takes the use of market leverage to win over consumers to your brand of product. Strategy is about creating and then exploiting leverage over an adversary or customer to achieve a goal.

So how are systems germane to the discussion of leverage? Systems can add to or subtract from the leverage you have over an opponent or a problem. The amount of leverage one has over an opponent comes from a few different sources. One source can be the superior raw power or size advantage one has over an opponent. For example, the United

States derives some leverage over Iran because of its military and economic superiority. But if raw power advantage automatically translated into leverage, Iran would have been less likely to rebuff U.S. efforts to resolve the current uranium enrichment issue. It appears that something else must be going on, for despite a raw power imbalance in favor of the United States, Iran refuses to budge.

What this tells us is that leverage dynamics are not solely driven by one party's superior raw power position. There are other significant sources of leverage that can offset or even trump the advantages one derives from raw power. This is where the importance of systems comes in. If an opponent seems immune to the attempts to exert leverage over it by a superior power, it is more than likely deriving additional leverage from some system in its external environment.

In the previous example, Iran gains significant leverage over the United States and Israel through alliances with Syria, Hezbollah, and Hamas, as well as its web of relationships in Iraq and Afghanistan, and it uses these to rebuff U.S. efforts to challenge it. This leverage comes partially from the specter that some of these allies will retaliate against U.S. and Israeli interests, should Iran ever be attacked. While these regional alliances have been severely attenuated as a result of the Arab Spring, they have not been completely undermined. Iran also derives leverage through its links to Russia and China in the broader international system, countries that vehemently oppose the use of military force against Iran.

It is the relationships within these regional and international systems that contribute to Iran's leverage and give it the flexibility to resist the pressure from the United States, despite having a weaker military and economic power position. Policymakers working on U.S. strategy for Iran need to understand how its leverage has been created and derived from these systems in its external environment. Otherwise, they will find that what were intended to be strategic moves in response to actions by the Iranians will yield only tactical advantages, making strategic success elusive.

WHAT ARE SYSTEMS?

Even though there is plenty of scholarly, theoretical work on systems, it is of limited value to the practitioner.[2] The trick is to sensitize practitioners to the fact that systems contribute to leverage without sending them down the rabbit hole of formal systems theory. For our purposes a system can be thought of as a web of relationships where a change in one part has an effect on the other parts.[3] Think about the human body system. Even though the body consists of individual organs, each of which performs its own function, the overall effect of the system is greater than the sum of these individual parts. Furthermore, changes in one organ can have an effect on the others, as well as the function of the overall human body.

There are systems as well in the social, political, economic, and business worlds. These systems have an effect on behavior that can't be explained solely by the actions of individual actors within it. Why do we need to refer to an abstraction like an industry to account for the performance and behavior of individual companies? Because the interactive dynamics that take place between suppliers, manufacturers, distributors, and retailers shape the options of companies competing in that industry. Companies can either benefit or suffer because of how power is distributed and how economics work in their respective industries. Changes in these dynamics either benefit or harm the ability of individual companies to compete, which means that the pull of the system we call an industry can shape a company's fortunes.

In the political world we refer to the international system, not merely as shorthand or a term of convenience, but as a way to capture political and economic properties that can't be explained solely by the actions of individual countries. We speak about the Middle East in regional terms because we understand that some behavior can only be understood by looking beyond the individual states. Thus, with a movement like the Arab Spring, a change to one country in the system can reverberate across the region and affect many other countries.

There are different types of systems, too. Formal systems have a defined organizational structure and leadership, within which actors have relative autonomy. These systems also have clear, objective boundaries, and there is little ambiguity as to who is, and who is not, contained within the system. Examples include political; economic or military alliances systems, like the EU and NATO; regional organizations like the Arab League; or business industry associations such as the National Association of Home Builders (NAHB) and the International Air Transport Association (IATA). Each of these systems has a modicum of organizational structure and defined leadership.

But in this chapter we will mostly be looking at informal systems, and while informal systems can form both inside and outside a country or business, our focus will be limited to systems of the external variety. In other words, for countries we won't be looking at the internal political systems of opponents; rather we will be looking at their external regional or international system environments. For businesses, we will be looking at industry systems, not the systems that form inside companies.

One important characteristic of informal systems of these types is that the boundaries are completely subjective. While some informal systems originate in a deliberate plan or through agreement, most often they emerge naturally and organically. Systems that develop organically have some discernible pattern of interaction or behaviors that emerge among actors. Because informal systems don't have any objective, natural boundaries, the strategist, like a surgeon defining and then draping off a surgical field, can circumscribe the boundaries based on circumstances at the time. That is, the strategist can somewhat arbitrarily decide where to demarcate the boundaries of the system.

One strategist might argue that when developing strategies for mitigating the Israeli-Palestinian conflict, the relevant system is the entire Arab Middle East and North Africa region, plus Iran and Turkey, while another might define a narrower system, consisting only of the conflict states of Syria, Jordan, Egypt, Lebanon, and Israel. On the business side, how should an airline like Southwest conceive of the boundaries of its industry system? Should it be defined narrowly as the U.S. airline industry, or more broadly as the global airline industry? Based on Southwest's current market footprint, it would be tenable to define it more narrowly as the U.S. airline industry. But if Southwest Airlines executives want to think further out into the future, considering possibilities for global expansion or a threat from foreign carriers entering the U.S. market, then they might define the industry environment in more global terms. Depending upon the magnitude of the goals being set, and the nature of the opponent, the boundaries of an informal system can be selectively adjusted by the strategist.

Look at Systems as Sources of Leverage

Political or business systems can either add to or subtract from the leverage of one's opponent. It is the job of the strategist to discern how external systems affect the opponent's leverage, and then develop strategies to disrupt that leverage. In order to analyze how a particular opponent derives leverage from its external systems environment the strategist needs to ask the following questions:

1. **Are there key *relationships* within the opponent's external system environment that either add to or subtract from its leverage?**

   Does the opponent derive leverage from specific alliances it has forged within its external environment, *and* are there detractors in the external environment that subtract from its leverage? If the answer is yes, then the follow-on question should be how important this set of relationships is to the opponent's leverage. In the case of alliances, if the relationship were interrupted, would the opponent's leverage decline significantly, or only an infinitesimal amount?

   In the case of detractors, would a sudden change in this relationship lead to an improvement in the opponent's leverage? What would have happened, for example, if China had disavowed North Korea in the wake of Kim Jong-Il's death? How instrumental has the political support North Korea receives from China been to its leverage vis-à-vis the United States? And if this support was disrupted, would this mean that North Korea's leverage over the United States on the nuclear issue would drop significantly?

   Businesses can also derive leverage over competitors through relationships with key suppliers or retailers within their industry system. The knowledge that a company is financially backed by a powerful customer, supplier, or investor may act as a deterrent to existing or would-be competitors who may consider challenging its market position. Alternatively, a hostile relationship with a key supplier or customer can make a company more vulnerable to competitive challenges. What will happen to AT&T's market leverage now that Apple has ended its exclusive relationship with the company? Will it make it more vulnerable to competitors like Verizon and Sprint, or is AT&T's leverage in the marketplace dependent on other factors?

2. **What are the key *properties* of the opponent's external system and how do these add to or subtract from its leverage?**

How does the system work? This requires the strategist to look beyond individual relationships to the broader horizon of the linkages within the system, how power is distributed within the system, and the patterns of interaction that make up the system. The strategist should be looking for how these system properties can positively or negatively affect the opponent's leverage. One should also ask how changes in those properties will likely affect the opponent's leverage. For example, how will the realignment of power in the Middle East regional system, in the wake of the collapse of radical Arab regimes of Saddam Hussein and Muammar Qaddafi, affect Iran's leverage vis-à-vis the United States? If Islamic parties continue to trump their secular counterparts in Tunisia, Egypt, Libya, and even possibly in Syria, will Iran's leverage be further enhanced, or will this be a threat to Iran's regional primacy? Also, what happens to Iran's leverage vis-à-vis the United States if its chain of linkages with Syria, Hezbollah, and Hamas get attenuated, or even truncated, by a collapse of the Assad government in Damascus? If a new Syrian government refuses to serve the intermediary role between Iran and the Lebanese group Hezbollah, what will the loss of this network mean for Iran's leverage vis-à-vis the United States?

On the business side, how do changes in the way an industry is structured affect companies operating within it? For example, how does the book industry's transition from a brick-and-mortar to an online business model affect the market leverage of booksellers like Barnes and Noble? In addition, how do the properties of the book industry constrain incumbents like Barnes and Noble from effectively competing with and prevailing over a new market challenger?[4] Will Barnes and Noble's industry system, and the business model developed therein, allow it to adapt to challenges from the outside like Amazon? Similarly, how did the structure of the cell phone industry affect Nokia's and Motorola's response to the challenge posed by Apple's launch of the iPhone in 2007? Was Nokia's and Motorola's inability to compete with Apple attributable to the misguided actions of these companies, or was this more a function of constraints imposed by properties of their industry structure? How did the fact that Nokia and Motorola outsourced their software, as was the industry standard, while Apple kept software and hardware design in-house, affect their ability to compete?[5]

3. **How does the opponent's geographic or physical *position* within its external system add to or subtract from its leverage?**

Iran, for example, derives a certain amount of leverage over the United States because of its close proximity to Iraq and Afghanistan. How does Iran's geostrategic position astride these two main venues of U.S. interests give it bargaining leverage? The fact that Iran, if provoked, could potentially stir up trouble in two countries whose stability the United States is trying to preserve, would have to be factored into any analysis of Iran's leverage. Also, how does Iran's strategic position in the Persian Gulf, an artery through which a large portion of oil flows, give it additional leverage over the United States?

Asking these three questions about how the opponent derives leverage from its external systems environment is essential to developing strategic responses for countering this leverage.[6]

DEVELOPING STRATEGIES IN THE DIMENSION OF SYSTEMS

While strategies that directly confront the opponent are likely to provoke an immediate and proportional response, indirect system strategies may go unnoticed by the opponent, or be perceived as less threatening if in fact they are noticed.[7] This means that system strategies are less likely to be met with hostility, careen out of control, or lead to a spiral of conflict, than strategies involving direct confrontation.[8] Because of this, they tend to be lower risk strategies.

But one would be remiss in regarding system strategies merely as risk free, conflict avoidance strategies. Indirect strategies generally complement, rather than replace, strategies aimed directly at an opponent, thereby increasing the probability of success if and when direct confrontation becomes necessary.[9] The idea is that by reducing the leverage the opponent receives from its external environment, indirect system strategy disadvantages it for any direct confrontation.[10] By tilting the leverage balance away from the opponent and making its external environment less hospitable, system strategies improve the chances that one will be successful in any confrontation.

Now let's focus on how strategists should look for opportunities to engage with an opponent's external environment in several different ways. The first is to disrupt relationships that yield leverage to the opponent, or to buttress relationships that yield leverage to you. Strategies can work on either side of the leverage ledger sheet, and the objective is to change the leverage dynamics in your favor. The second way to target the opponent's external environment is to disrupt the properties of the system that benefit the opponent. Here the idea is to transform a nourishing external environment into a threatening environment for the opponent. The final way to target the opponent's external environment is to undermine its positioning advantages, by either weakening its leadership position or blocking the effects of favorable geographic positioning.

Before going further, it is important to address the fact that system strategies have to clear two main hurdles. The first is that the strategy has to influence the opponent's external environment in the intended way. Remember that the idea of these types of strategies is to attenuate the support, ties, and leverage the opponent derives from its external environment. The strategist will need to be confident that his or her actions will get the opponent's allies, and the broader system environment itself, to act in the desired way.

The second hurdle is that, assuming that you are successful in influencing the opponent's external environment, this influence must translate into a profound reduction of leverage on the part of the opponent. The strategist must be confident that the changes in the opponent's system environment will influence its behavior. Like in billiards, where hitting the first ball needs to propel the second ball towards the pocket, system strategies need to be able to actually influence the behavior and decisions of the opponent.

Given the complexity of these types of strategies, there is likely to be a great deal of uncertainty about clearing these two hurdles. Like in billiards, where the slightest miscalculation can lead to failure to pocket the ball, one misstep in system strategies can produce catastrophic results.

Strategists need to explicate their assumptions about why, given this uncertainty, they believe their actions will influence the opponent's system, and how this in turn will influence the opponent's decisions.

Strategies Aimed at Relationships within the System

This section will address specific strategies for using relationships with other actors in the system to alter leverage dynamics against an opponent by either disrupting the opponent's relationships or adapting to them.

Disrupting the Opponent's Relationships

There are some relationships that are immutable and resistant to change. Alliances between countries and partnerships among businesses may be cemented by a web of mutual interests that are virtually bulletproof to attempts from the outside to weaken them. Sometimes these mutual interests are fortified by an ideological or cultural affinity, for example, the relationship between the United States and Israel. While there are mutual strategic interests that bind these two countries, the real glue is the political support Israel enjoys within the U.S. government. Although the bonds between these two allies may become frayed, it is unlikely that their relationship could be successfully disrupted by the strategy of a third party.

But relationships like this are the exception rather than the rule. The relationships a business or government has with other actors in its external environment are probably based largely on mutual interests and this is what becomes the target of the strategist. Any strategy that targets the relationships of the opponent will need to focus on changing the way its allies calculate their interests. The idea will be to alter the way the ally perceives its interests vis-à-vis the opponent, or to create new interests that trump the interests binding it to the opponent.

This means that the target of your strategy has to be chosen very carefully. One way is to identify the low hanging fruit, which are relationships where there might already be some instability or vulnerability. That may be a relationship where the bonds are created more by short-term convenience than longer-term mutual interests. Or, it may be a case where relationships bound by some set of long-term mutual interests are already fraying and therefore vulnerable to outside influence. The strategist also needs to be sensitive to the higher hanging fruit, which are relationships where the glue of mutual interests is still strong, but where intervention might alter how those interests are perceived and prioritized. As tight as those relationships are, the use of incentives or threats could actually undermine them.

Let's look at a business example where one company sabotaged the partnership of a competitor by undermining the interests that were the glue of the relationship. FedEx's strategy to disrupt Airborne Express's strategic alliance with Roadway Package System (RPS) is illustrative of how to loosen the glue of an opponent's relationship, and how to make this work to one's own competitive advantage. In this case, FedEx created a new set of interests for RPS, undermining its partnership with Airborne.

Airborne Express had been a long standing competitor of FedEx, focusing primarily on businesses that ship packages regularly by air to other businesses. This was in contrast to FedEx, which also had a large residential delivery service. Airborne observed two things about its competitive environment. The first was that FedEx was likely going to add a ground package delivery service to its thriving air service. They realized that if FedEx offered both ground and air services, it could potentially put Airborne at a competitive disadvantage. The second thing it observed was that in tough economic times FedEx, and rival UPS, would try to grab additional revenue by targeting Airborne's business-to-business market niche.

In a defensive move designed to protect itself from these threats, Airborne decided to augment its air express service with a new ground package delivery service, similar to what was being considered by Fed Ex, and what was already offered by UPS. As part of this strategic initiative, Airborne forged an alliance in 1995 with RPS, a company that was already starting to make competitive inroads against UPS in the ground package delivery market. Airborne calculated that starting a ground service from scratch wasn't viable, but an alliance with RPS would give them quicker, and cheaper, traction in the market. While the plan never called for Airborne and RPS to merge their operations, the alliance did call for the two companies to co-market to their clients by bundling the air and ground services they offered into a packaged deal.

The relationship between Airborne and RPS had been built on mutual interests. Airborne saw an opportunity to broaden the products it could offer to its core base of customers, fortifying it against what was perceived to be an inevitable competitive onslaught from FedEx and UPS. RPS saw the opportunity to combine its growing ground delivery service with Airborne's robust air express service to businesses, strengthening its overall market position as well.

The problems started for Airborne when its alliance with RPS elicited a countermove by the more powerful and better heeled FedEx, who began to woo and ultimately acquire RPS in 1997. Even though the partnership between Airborne and RPS had been built on mutual interests, FedEx successfully altered RPS's calculation of interests, cutting Airborne's strategy off at the knees.

How was this possible given the mutual interests that bound RPS to Airborne? It happened because FedEx shifted the interests of the management team at Caliber Systems, RPS's parent company. As mutually beneficial as the RPS-Airborne deal was, it was viewed as somewhat speculative by RPS and its parent Caliber Systems. The partnership wasn't built on a certainty of success, or with a clear financial exit strategy for the RPS management team. Rather it was built on optimistic assumptions about what the future held and the unproven proposition that the combined offering of Airborne and RPS would fuel the growth of both companies. By contrast, the FedEx deal was a clean buy-out, complete with cash and FedEx stock for the RPS management team. In effect, the certainty the deal offered to Caliber and RPS undermined the mutuality of interests between RPS and Airborne.

FedEx ultimately transformed the newly acquired RPS into today's FedEx Ground, which is an integral part of the overall FedEx product offering. This pushed Airborne into a very lonely and disadvantageous strategic corner in the market. In an attempt to break out of its strategic isolation, Airborne struck a partnership with the United States Postal Service in 1999, a move that generated little strategic traction. However, Airborne was unable to fully recover from FedEx's move and, in 2003, sold its shares to the global shipping company DHL.[11]

So what is the lesson we should take from this case about the ability to disrupt relationships based on strong mutual interests? While less powerful actors might be able to disrupt a relationship of a more powerful opponent, this type of move is generally reserved for more powerful actors like FedEx. It seems unlikely that Airborne as underdog could have successfully prevailed in a bidding war to prevent the merger between FedEx and RPS, or that it could have strengthened the terms of its partnership agreement sufficiently to forestall RPS's deal with FedEx.

While the previous example dealt with a situation where a relationship was built on strong mutual interests, strategy can also be used to disrupt alliances built on short-term convenience, or where the mutuality of interests is already fraying. Take, for example, when the United States disrupted Iraq's fraying relationships in the lead up to the first Gulf War.

Iraq's relationships with its Arab neighbors were forged during its war with Iran, which it initiated in 1980. Saudi Arabia, Kuwait, and Jordan reluctantly supported Iraq, while Syria steadfastly sided with Iran. The reticence on the part of Saudi Arabia, Kuwait, and Jordan was because Saddam Hussein had proven to be a volatile, unpredictable regional bully, inclined to use incendiary and threatening language toward the monarchies in the region. But with the war shifting in Iran's favor in 1982, along with growing fears about what an Iranian victory would mean for the region, the aforementioned Arab states, the Soviet Union, and the United States, all moved toward a firm backing of Iraq.

At the end of hostilities in 1988, these relationships began to fray when Iraq tried to portray the Iran-Iraq war as an Arab-Persian conflict, implying that debts incurred by Iraq from Saudi Arabia and Kuwait during the war should be forgiven. Tensions mounted when Iraq threatened both Saudi Arabia and Kuwait with aggression. Most leaders in the region believed that the Iraqi threats were mere bravado, and that an invasion of Kuwait was not imminent. They were wrong; Iraqi forces attacked and annexed Kuwait in 1990.

Although the United States hesitated at first, it quickly mobilized a coalition against Iraq. In doing so, it disrupted almost all of Iraq's Arab relationships, except for Jordan. The coalition, which consisted of U.S. Western allies, Arab states, and Pakistan, was created to weaken Iraq politically and militarily. The coup for the United States was getting Arab states from all ideological stripes to join the alliance.

But what was strategically significant was that the coalition included countries like Egypt and Saudi Arabia, which had previously supported Iraq. By exploiting the vulnerability in the fraying relationships between Iraq and its Arab allies, the United States was able to gain huge strategic dividends.

Some might argue that this was no real strategic feat for the United States given the fact that Syria had already indirectly battled Iraq by siding with Iran during the Iran-Iraq war, and that Saudi Arabia's participation in the coalition was motivated by fear that Saddam Hussein, if successful in swallowing Kuwait, would turn its sights on the kingdom. But this overlooks what it took to get countries, which had only privately and passively been seething at Saddam's brutish behavior, to publicly and actively form a coalition with the United States. It also overlooks the political risk taken by the Arab countries in joining a U.S.-led battle against a fellow Arab state. Each country incurred some costs in terms of political legitimacy by backing the United States. Saudi Arabia, and to some degree Egypt, took domestic political heat, and although they were able to control the backlash, there was discontent from militant Islamic groups in both countries. Moreover, both countries incurred significant financial burden in the conflict—Saudi Arabia had bankrolled much of the effort, and in the aftermath of the conflict, Egypt sought assistance from the International Monetary Fund partially to offset the costs of the war.

So, putting together this coalition and disrupting Iraq's relationships was a significant achievement. While it exploited the fears of Arab leaders in the region, it nonetheless represented a diplomatic victory for the United States. Unlike FedEx, which disrupted the interests that bound Airborne and RPS by creating new and even greater opportunities for RPS, the United States undermined Iraq's relationships by playing to the Arab countries' perception of threat.

This begs the question of how including Saudi Arabia, the United Arab Emirates, Egypt, Qatar, Oman, and Syria in the coalition increased the leverage the United States had over Iraq. In this case, the real contribution was more political than military. While Saddam Hussein portrayed these countries as "defectors" from the Arab cause and as stooges of the United States, the inclusion of Arab states helped give the United States the leverage it needed to get an authorization for the use of force from the United Nations. It also gave the United States the international legitimacy it needed to successfully wage the war and evict Iraq from Kuwait.

The question remaining is whether the two aforementioned cases cleared the two hurdles of strategies in the dimension of systems. The first hurdle is to successfully disrupt the relationship between the opponent and its allies. In both the case of FedEx vs. Airborne and the U.S. vs. Iraq, the efforts to disrupt the relationships of the opponent were successful. The Airborne-RPS relationship was upended by FedEx's bid to acquire RPS, and the United States successfully convinced the Arab states to become part of the coalition against Iraq. In each of these cases, the mechanism that caused the disruption was some form of positive inducement. In the case of RPS it was the financial exit strategy provided by FedEx, and for the Arabs it was mitigation of the threat perceived by a volatile and jingoistic Saddam Hussein.

The second and always tougher hurdle is to demonstrate the strategic significance of these disruptions. In other words, what impact did the altered relationship have on the leverage of the opponent? In both cases, the causal links are quite clear. Both the FedEx acquisition of RPS and the cooperation of the Arab States, and their inclusion in the U.S.-led coalition, had dramatic impact on the ultimate outcomes. In response to the preemptive move by FedEx, Airborne scurried to form a strategically ineffective relationship with the U.S. Postal Service, and ultimately sold to DHL. The United States was able to successfully roll back Iraqi forces from Kuwait, while fortifying its Arab allies in the region. As we will see in future examples, the causal link between system strategies and the behavior of the opponent can be difficult to prove, but in the cases we just addressed, the impact seems reasonably clear.

Forming Relationships to
Counterbalance an Opponent's Leverage

There will be times when disrupting the relationships that give the opponent leverage is either impossible or fraught with significant risk. Relationships may be resistant to change, and attempts to disrupt them can lead to unintended negative consequences. For this reason, these types of strategies are generally best suited to situations where a powerful actor is trying to reduce the leverage of a less powerful opponent. This was certainly the case with FedEx's face-off against Airborne, and the United States confrontation with Iraq. But it doesn't mean that strategies aren't available to smaller actors facing off against more powerful adversaries. There are strategies for altering the leverage dynamics against a more powerful actor that don't entail the risk of disrupting their relationships.

One approach is to forge an alliance with another actor in order to counterbalance the leverage created by the more powerful actor. The idea is to look for partners whose interests align with yours regarding your opponent. These kinds of strategies can be effective in narrowing the leverage deficiency for strong and weak actors alike, as they can counteract the effect of an opponent's relationships by forming their own coalitions. Let's look at both business and national security examples.

The phenomenon of businesses trying to counteract the advantages of a competitor by merging with another company is quite common. The series of mergers and acquisitions that swept the oil and gas industry between 1998 and 2002 was perpetuated by major oil companies adapting to the merger activity of their competitors. Exxon responded to the merger between its rivals BP and Amoco by acquiring Mobil, forming the Exxon-Mobil Corporation. Only four months later, BP responded with its own countermove by purchasing Los Angeles-based Atlantic Richfield Company (ARCO).[12] This maneuvering represented attempts by each oil giant to counteract the consolidation moves of the other. Since they couldn't disrupt their competitor's mergers, they tried to gain market advantages through their own merger relationships. Each of these moves and counter moves was built on an understanding that market leverage is gained over an opponent by making oneself bigger and more powerful through merger partners.

Countries, too, try to counteract relationships formed by rivals by forming coalitions of their own. Syria's relationship with Iran is a good example of this. Part of what has perpetuated this alliance with Iran has been a perceived need to counterbalance what Syria sees as threatening coalitions among its adversaries.

Syria's relationship with Iran goes back to the early 1980s, when it became the only Arab country to align with Iran during the Iran-Iraq War. While there were several factors that explained this strange relationship between the predominantly Sunni, Arab Syria and predominantly Shi'i, non-Arab Iran, Syria's longstanding rivalry with Iraq was a major one. The Iran-Iraq war gave Syria the opportunity to weaken its most formidable regional nemesis through an alliance with Iran. After the cessation of hostilities, Syria's relationship with Iran deepened and solidified further. Much of this had to do with Syria's perception of threat from the west, and a need to adapt to this by fortifying its own alliances. After the Cold War and the demise of the Soviet Union, Syria again found itself at a strategic disadvantage against Israel and the West. Having lost its superpower benefactor, the Soviet Union, and the regional leverage this relationship provided, Syria was thrust into a geopolitically vulnerable position. The Cold War had created a sort of artificial symmetry in the leverage balance between Syria and Israel; its end meant that Israel retained the leverage benefits that accompanied its relationship with the United States, while Syria lost what it had with the Soviet Union.

To redress this power imbalance against its adversaries, Syria deepened its ties with Iran, fortified its bonds to the Lebanese Shi'i group, Hezbollah, and later became a benefactor to the Palestinian group Hamas. These relationships gave Syria the strategic significance it needed with Israel. They also gave Syria some leverage against what was perceived to be an increasingly hostile United States. Syria felt quite vulnerable and threatened after the United States entered Iraq in 2003, particularly in light of the fact that the Bush administration had designated it as part of the "axis of evil" one year earlier. To counteract its disadvantaged leverage position relative to the United States and Israel, Syria fortified its bonds with Iran. These bonds remain strong to this day, with Iran being the only country in the region to forcefully back the Assad regime as it comes under siege from rebels determined to see it overthrown.[13]

These strategies may be used by powerful and not-so-powerful organizations and states. Multinational corporations might pursue mergers and alliances in response to the actions of its largest competitors, for example. But these types of strategies are particularly important for governments and businesses facing powerful opponents. In these situations adapting to an opponent's alliances by creating one's own can spell the difference between survival and defeat.

Strategies Aimed at the Properties of the System

Up to this point we have focused on ways to reduce the leverage of an opponent by disrupting the relationships they have within their external environment or forming counterbalancing alliances. Now we will consider strategies that focus less on the individual relationships and more on the broader system within which those relationships take place. This will require us to raise our sights above the level of bilateral relationships, and instead take aim at the properties of the external systems themselves. These high level strategies will try to reduce the leverage of the opponent by breaking the links between the system and the opponent, in effect isolating the opponent. They will focus on disrupting the benefits the opponent derives from the way their external system environment works. For governments this means that one state tries to disrupt the benefits the opponent derives from its regional or international political system. For businesses this means that one company tries to prevail over a competitor by adapting to or shaping the structure of its industry.

Adapting to System Properties

Strategies that adapt to the opponent's systemic environment shouldn't automatically be construed as passive, defensive, or originating in positions of weakness. In fact they can often involve offensive actions. As we will tease out through the examples that follow, while these strategies are adaptive, they try to gain advantage over an opponent by aggressively exploiting gaps, weaknesses, vulnerabilities, or other properties of the system. They can also work by exploiting a system trend, so rather than trying to change the system itself, they work by making the system inhospitable to the opponent.

Adapting to System Gaps

Let's begin by exploring how leverage against an adversary can be created by exploiting gaps in systems. Earlier in this chapter we drew the distinction between different types of systems. Formal systems are deliberately formed and somewhat hierarchical in nature. In contrast, informal systems tend to lack any master design, but instead tend to evolve organically over time. Because of the lack of formal structure in these systems, there may be gaps that can be exploited to compromise the leverage of an adversary. In addition, the lack of any formal governance structures over informal systems means that these voids may be undefended and therefore relatively easy to exploit. Gaps in markets, known as niches, can be filled by companies trying to establish a beachhead from which to attack a more established competitor. Sovereignty gaps in political systems can be exploited by weak actors trying to create leverage and competitive advantage over stronger actors.

The following are a couple of business and national security examples involving the creation of leverage by exploiting gaps in the systems environment. First we'll look at the strategic situation faced by violent non-state actors like the Somali Pirates, who exploited voids in the international system.

During the Cold War the alliances between the superpowers and their dependent client states imbued the international system with a semblance of structure. When the Cold War ended, the structure provided by this bipolar set of alliances collapsed, leaving fragile states fraught with civil conflict in its wake. These states had barely functioning governments, causing sovereignty gaps in the international system. Globalization had ensured that the fortunes of rich and poor countries were interdependent in a number of ways, but the political structures seemed to lag behind the reality of economic interdependence. So, while the structure of the international political system frayed, the interconnectedness of the economic system increased. The new gaps in the international political system could now be exploited.

One of the features of this new system was the emergence of violent non-state actors equipped with relatively meager resources that could prey on and exploit these fragile, loosely governed states. The Somali Pirates exploited holes in the functioning of the system to their own benefit. They took advantage of the fact that the imperatives of global trade made commercial travel in the Indian Ocean and Arabian Sea a necessity. They also exploited the weakness and lawlessness of Somalia to attack and extort money from shipping companies. Moreover, they took advantage of the lack of police functions on the high seas and of the fact that Somalia is incapable of patrolling either its littoral or land borders. While they adapted to, rather than created, their broader environment, they exploited it to give themselves leverage against Western commercial interests. Whether the actions of the pirates are truly strategic or merely tactical will depend on how agile they become in adapting to improved patrolling of the seas and to defensive measures taken by shipping and insurance companies. By exploiting gaps in the international system, small groups like the Somali pirates, and certainly more powerful actors like al-Qaeda, can turn an international system, which in many ways served the interests of the United States, into a significant threat. But, the broader lesson is that an understanding of the properties of systems, and how to spot their vulnerabilities, can be used to create competitive advantage.

Businesses also can exploit holes in their external systems environments. These external systems can be the broader international political systems, like in the case of companies that take advantage of gaps in international regulatory environments. They can also be industry systems, like when new companies emerge in response to unfilled market gaps or niches. Niche strategies come about when companies believe there are underserved market segments, or unmet consumer needs. Companies pursuing these kinds of strategies adapt their business model to turn these market or industry gaps into opportunities.

The 7-Eleven convenience store chain is an example of a company that emerged using niche strategy. When the company, which formed in 1927, changed its name to 7-Eleven in 1946 there was a trend underfoot in the United States of populations moving from urban areas to the suburbs. With this demographic trend came retail trends, like the emergence and popularity of large supermarkets. The supermarket format was well suited for customers making their main weekly food-shopping trip—once a week customers would travel some distance to go to a large supermarket, contend with lines, parking issues, and traffic, to bulk up on their groceries. But the owners of 7-Eleven felt the emergence of the supermarket created a gap in the industry. They saw an unfilled customer need to be able to make small, intermittent purchases, without the hassle of driving to, and then navigating through, a large store. They believed there was a demand for a store that would be closer, more convenient, and open later than the supermarket.

The emergence of the large supermarket transformed the retail industry and in the process created an opportunity for convenience store entrepreneurs. 7-Eleven was built on the premise of being a local neighborhood alternative to the larger supermarket, whose customers were willing to pay higher prices for certain products based on convenience.[14] Their success came because they adapted to the existing industry system by identifying and then filling gaps they saw.

So the lesson for strategists is to look for opportunity in undefended, undeveloped, or unexplored areas of their external systems environments and then adapt to, or exploit, any gaps they find. These opportunities might come because of gaps in the structures of the systems themselves, as was the case with the Somali pirates.. Or, they might arise because the creation of new structures, like the emergence of the supermarket, leads to potential new forms of demand.

Adapting to Trends in the System

Political and business systems are never static; they are dynamic and evolving continuously. The strategist should be sensitive to and look for ways to adapt to trends in how these systems are evolving. These types of adaptation strategies, while not limited to weak actors, may be the only option for organizations or countries lacking the resources or power to transform their opponent's environments. Rather than expending valuable political or financial capital trying to change the environment, weaker organizations can try to spot and then ride a wave of change that is already occurring.

Let's look at a foreign policy and a business case, both of which involve situations where strategy was used to adapt to what were perceived to be favorable trends. The foreign policy example shows the strategy of the Palestinians in their quest for independence. The 2011 bid by Palestinian Authority president Mahmoud Abbas for the United Nations (UN) to grant state status to Palestine was based on the belief that there were exploitable positive trends in the international system. One of those trends was an intensifying perception in the international community that the Israeli-Palestinian issue had the potential to further destabilize the international political system. This feeling was supported by the 2009 comment by European Union (EU) foreign policy chief Javier Solana that the UN should mandate a solution to the conflict should Israel and Palestine to fail to break the deadlock.[15] The implication was that the conflict was no longer just a regional issue, but had now blossomed into a significant threat to international security.

Palestinian leaders also believed that there was an increased perception in the international community that Israelis, as opposed to the Palestinians, represented the major obstacle to peace. They also saw the rise of populist movements of the Arab Spring as generally favorable to their cause. While there was little evidence that an Arab Spring-like Palestinian uprising was imminent, Abbas saw an opportunity to exploit this, believing that the specter of greater instability in the Arab world, and the possibility that a deadlock on the Israel-Palestine issue could create instability in the West Bank, would get the international community to act. Abbas hoped that these trends would give the Palestinian Authority a shot of getting at least some support for statehood in the UN Security Council. Abbas submitted an application at the opening of the General Assembly meeting on September 23, 2011, believing that even if the Security Council voted against Palestinian statehood, the move would gain traction in the General Assembly. While the Security Council bid for statehood failed in 2011 due to the veto by the United States, in 2012 the General Assembly in a 138–50 vote conferred non-member observer state status on Palestine.

Abbas's theory was that under any circumstances, Palestinian's bargaining leverage against Israel would be enhanced. The logic behind his strategy was that while Israel's superior power gave it leverage to resist any serious bilateral negotiations with the Palestinians, the trends mentioned previously provided the Palestinians an opportunity to leverage support from the international system. In the wake of the breakdown of peace talks between Israel and the Palestinians, sponsored by U.S. president Barack Obama, in Washington, D.C., in 2010, President Abbas considered unilaterally announcing an independent state. But he felt that more pressure could be brought to bear on Israel by first seeking UN statehood status.[16] While fraught with considerable risk and uncertainty, it is an example of a strategy of riding the coattails of what are thought to be favorable trends.

There are examples of companies that have developed robust strategies of adapting to trends in the environment, as well. Pharmaceutical giant Eli Lilly's foray into India is illustrative in this regard. The company entered the Indian market in the 1990s, almost two decades after most of its global competitors. Lilly's market entry was timed to take advantage of an emerging trend toward political and economic liberalization in India. For the previous two decades there had been no patent protection in India, and the government had controlled prices on pharmaceuticals. Because of these inhospitable macro and industry conditions, Lilly had consciously decided to stay out of the market. Most of Lilly's competitors entered the Indian market anyway, selling generic or off-patent products while keeping their prized patented drugs out of the market.

But in the 1990s India wanted to become a member of the World Trade Organization (WTO), so it began loosening its draconian control over prices and started to recognize patents on pharmaceuticals. Lilly saw this new trend toward openness and liberalization and it gave them confidence that real change was afoot and that the prospects for a robust pharmaceutical industry in India were good. Thus, the company developed an entry strategy around this trend. In other words, they aimed their strategy not at where the environment was, but instead at where it was heading.

How did this strategy give Eli Lilly leverage against the already entrenched competition that presumably had first mover advantages? The company capitalized on the fact that their competition had developed business models around, and had sunken costs in, the old protectionist Indian system. Lilly could hit the ground running with a winning business model, while the others would have to rebuild their organizations around a new emerging reality. By choosing to enter the Indian market at the beginning of a new trend, Lilly was able to turn last mover status into an advantage. The company had to execute the strategy well, but they let the trends in the environment do much of the work for them. As liberalization continued, Eli Lilly's model worked to its advantage and to the disadvantage of the entrenched competition. Their analysis of trends and the ensuing strategy of adaption gave them incredible competitive advantage over their most formidable competitors.[17]

Adapting by Riding the Coattails of More Powerful Actors

Riding the wave of a general trend is one way to adapt to the current external systems environment. But another way to adapt is to link one's strategy to the efforts of a more powerful actor within that system. This is not to say that strategy should ever be outsourced. Success will still depend on how well you design and execute your strategy. But it is possible to get greater results than might otherwise be possible by pointing your strategy into the tailwind of a more powerful actor.

Newell Corporation, a company that sold decorative hardware and building products to retail outlets is a good example from the business perspective. In the company's early history, it struggled with a growth strategy in what was a very fragmented industry. While the retailers that were the company's existing customers, and the bread and butter of its business, were independent hardware stores and lumberyards, Newell's management saw the growth of large discount retailers as a trend that would shake up the industry. But unlike Newell's existing customers, who saw the growth of the discount chains as a threat, Newell saw this trend as an opportunity. They understood that this was a trend that couldn't be reversed or fought and believed that the growth of a few large retail chains would threaten the survival of the company's coterie of distributors—independent lumberyards and hardware stores.

Instead of fighting this trend, Newell's strategy was to capitalize on the growth trajectories of more powerful players, such as mega-retailer K-Mart, and later Home Depot and Wal-Mart. Newell pointed its strategy away from the independent distributors and hardware stores, instead focusing on becoming a supplier to these mega-chains. The strategy involved developing the technology, scale, and product assortment required to service the needs of these mass retailers. They offered the large retailer a one-stop place to shop for a whole range of building products—from faucets to curtain rods to painting equipment. Moreover, the company's success depended on its capacity to keep up with the meteoric growth of these fast moving chains. Newell invested in the technology and systems that made it an indispensible partner to the emerging chains. It also invested in marketing and merchandising systems, which facilitated the sale of Newell products through the chain stores.

Newell Corporation switched from a strategy of catering to the needs of small independent lumberyards and hardware stores to one of selling to the mass retail merchant. It calculated that the trend toward the strengthening of the national retail chains at the expense of the small, independent retailer was inexorable. It also calculated that there was more opportunity than risk for the company in this trend, so it made the bold move of hitching its future to the fortunes of the rising large retailer.[18]

This type of adaptation strategy is not limited to businesses. In the global economic system, small countries can hitch a ride on the strategies of more powerful countries that are leading change in the international system. Australia followed this kind of adaptation strategy, using its hosting of the 2000 Winter Olympics as an opportunity to capitalize on the trend of a rising China.

Australia's leaders had already acknowledged that the country's status as a destination market for global companies had been undermined by the emergence of larger market opportunities in China. It was clear that there was no way to compete against China as a market for foreign direct investors. So rather than trying to fight this, Australian leaders decided to use strategy to turn an unavoidable, potentially negative trend into a positive outcome for the country. Using the visibility and publicity provided by the 2000 Olympics, they decided to promote Australia not as a central, stand-alone market, but rather as a secure and stable spot that could house the distribution, sales, and technology functions of companies serving the burgeoning Chinese markets.

The strategy worked because companies going to China were reluctant, out of concerns about political risk, to concentrate all of their infrastructure assets in that country. Australia served as a way for these global companies to reduce their political risk exposure. So, rather than fighting the trend of a rising China, Australia hitched a ride on the country's growth.[19] It is a classic example of how a negative leverage position can be turned into a positive position using strategies of adaptation.

Both the Newell and Australia cases demonstrate the possibility of aligning one's strategy with the strategic direction of a more powerful actor in order to create competitive advantage. In both instances the strategy involved turning what could have been a strategic disadvantage at the hands of more powerful actors, into strategic advantage. While there was always a risk that the big retail chains or China could change course and undermine Newell's and Australia's strategies, respectively, the risks were outweighed by the opportunities.

Shaping System Properties

Up to this point we have been examining strategies that adapt to, rather than shape, the properties of the opponent's external system environment. These strategies accept the reality of the current system and create strategic advantage by adapting to them. Now we will turn our attention to the higher-stake strategies that entail shaping the opponent's external systems environment. Changing a system that provides bargaining leverage to an opponent into an inhospitable environment can be the key to strategic success. It can help create the multiplier effect that is so important in any strategic endeavor.

The use of these strategies presupposes several things. The first is that there is sufficient capability to catalyze the desired system change and to parlay that change into bargaining leverage. Small states and businesses may have the ability to disrupt the status quo but may lack the capacity to convert this into strategic advantage. That is, they may not be able to turn disruption of the system into leverage. Terrorist organizations, for example, may have the capacity to disrupt the international system but tend to be less adept at shaping it in a particular direction. As we will see in chapter 6, however, al-Qaeda may be an exception to this general rule.

The second assumption is that the benefit of fomenting change in the environment outweighs the potential risk. In other words, it has to be clear that the potential upside of the strategy is great enough to justify possible downsides and the risk of unintended consequences. One could say that the Bush administration didn't properly analyze the risk of disrupting the status quo in Iraq in 2003. Their assumption was that they had both the capacity to disrupt the old system and shape a new better one. While they were correct with the former, they may yet be proven wrong with the latter.[20]

Unfortunately there is no universal playbook for developing system shaping strategies. But there are some general types of strategies that should be useful to the practitioner. The first type involves disrupting the current system so as to disadvantage the opponent. The second type involves strengthening a property of the system that can redound to your advantage. The third type involves changing the competitive dynamics completely by creating an entirely new system. All of these different approaches work by altering the competitive dynamics for the opponent by changing the nature of its external systems environment.

Disrupting System Properties

In cases where the opponent derives clear leverage from its external systems environment, strategies that adapt to this reality may not be effective. In these cases the strategist might be faced with the imperative of trying to disrupt the opponent's benefits, isolating it by cutting the ties between it and its supportive external environment.

The case of the relationship between the United States and Iran is a good example. As previously discussed, despite Iran's relative raw power disadvantage and smaller size, it has been effective in generating sufficient leverage to rebuff the United States on the nuclear issue. Iran derived this leverage both from actions it took and from the windfall of U.S. misfortunes in Iraq and Afghanistan. It painstakingly built a web of relationships in the Middle East regional system, which contributed to its leverage. These relationships were constructed in such as way as to maximize Iran's strategic depth, giving it the ability to project power and influence right into the conflict zones of the region.

Beginning in the early 1980s the revolutionary government of Iran built a strong political, economic, and ideological relationship with the Lebanese Shi'i group Hezbollah. In fact, Iran was responsible for the group's formation. With Hezbollah as a client, Iran gained the ability to influence events in Lebanon, indirectly create mischief on Israel's sensitive northern border, and challenge U.S. interests in the region. Today, Iran also funds and arms the Gaza-based group Islamic Jihad, and until very recently it supported the Palestinian group Hamas. Iran's non-state partners have provided leverage by giving it a credible retaliatory capability should the United States or Israel try to take out Iran's nuclear facilities.

But any analysis of Iran's system of leverage that omits Syria's role with Iran would be remiss. Syria has become the linchpin of Iran's strategy, serving as the intermediary link between Iran and its network of non-state actors. It became an efficient and easy channel through which Iran supplied Hezbollah with arms, training, and funds. To a lesser degree Syria was also a conduit connecting Iran with Hamas and Islamic Jihad. Although the influence Syria has over Hezbollah has been compromised since Syria left Lebanon in 2005 and the Assad regime became besieged during the Arab Spring, it continues to perform an important conduit function for Iran.

Is there a plausible strategy for the United States to disrupt the properties of this system of influence so artfully designed by Iran? In other words, is there a way to attenuate if not completely undermine Iran's relationships with the radical groups Hezbollah and Hamas, both of which have the ability to threaten U.S. and Israeli interests? In 2010 the Obama administration attempted to woo Syria away from its alliance with Iran using economic and political inducements. While this move didn't assume that Iran's relationships with Hamas and Hezbollah would be terminated, the idea was to weaken Iran's critical link to these radical groups by coopting Syria. Had the approach worked before the

Assad regime came under siege, an interruption of Syria's function as intermediary link would undermine the credibility of Iran's claim that these radical groups would retaliate against U.S. and Israeli interests in the Mediterranean, if Iran were attacked.

Remember that any disruption strategy has to clear two hurdles. The first is that it has to actually disrupt the system of the opponent, and the second is that this disruption must actually compromise the opponent's leverage. Prior to the Arab Spring, what would have made a U.S. strategist confident that Syria could be drawn away from its alliance with Iran, such that the properties of the system would be compromised? Prior to the eruption of the Arab Spring, there were some positive signs in this regard. In 2009 it appeared that Damascus was looking for a way out of its isolation and might be open to better relations with the United States. Part of this was motivated by economics and part by Syria's enduring goal of regaining control over the Golan Heights, something it lost to Israel in the 1967 war.[21] To be clear, Syria never showed any willingness to jettison its alliance with Iran. But there were signs that Syria might be easing itself back into the international system.

In the midst of the Arab Spring, this strategic option is obviously off the table. The United States has issued several strong, diplomatic demarches against the Syrian government, including calling for President Bashar Assad to step down. But perhaps the changes that are now sweeping Syria and the region could accomplish what U.S. strategy alone couldn't. Depending on how things play out, it is possible that either the Assad government or its successor regime will need to reassess its alliances and regional interests, including the relationship with Iran. If Iran loses Syria either by the dint of U.S. diplomacy or the dynamics of the Arab Spring, it has lost a significant connection to the rest of the region. This loss could certainly have consequences for Iran's leverage. Among other things it could reduce Iran's strategic depth and undermine the part of Iran's retaliatory capability that rested with Hezbollah and Hamas.[22] If that is the case, then the second hurdle of compromising Iran's leverage will be cleared.

Now we will focus on a business example of how disrupting system linkages can disadvantage an opponent. Shortly after Michael Dell started Dell Computer, he recognized that the only way to win against competitors such as IBM, Compaq, and HP was to disrupt the properties of the personal computer industry, rather than to adapt to it. He concluded that the profits of companies that manufactured computers were getting squeezed both by suppliers and retailers, and that it was difficult for a computer manufacturer to make money within the existing industry structure. On the supply chain side, Intel and Microsoft had been putting pressure on industry margins, while, on the distribution channel side, mass retailers such as CompUSA were also flexing their buying power muscles and putting downward pressure on profits. Dell saw how futile it would be to try to adapt his company to this economically inhospitable environment. He also saw that it made little economic sense to compete with the other manufacturers on the basis of price, due to current industry margins.

So instead of competing head-to-head with the other companies, he began changing the rules of the computer industry. Historically, personal computer manufacturers had sold to distributors, resellers, and retailers, which in turn sold to end-user businesses and consumers. Breaking with industry practices, Dell sold computers directly to consumers and businesses, disintermediating the industry's traditional distribution channel. By doing this he captured profits that would otherwise have gone to retailers and distributors, and placed his competitors, which found it difficult to jettison their relationships with existing distributors and retailers, at a severe disadvantage.

In addition to capturing more profits, selling direct also brought Dell closer to its customers. This enabled the company to customize their products for different market segments and around individual customer needs, which helped increase demand and led to Dell's meteoritic growth. The increased profitability that came from direct market selling and increased demand for its products gave Dell the market leverage it needed to become the industry leader. By tinkering with the industry structure, Dell became the most formidable competitor in the industry.[23] While it still competed directly with IBM and the others in the marketplace, its real competitive advantage came from the indirect move of changing the industry's structure to make it work to its advantage and to the disadvantage of the competition. In fact IBM sold its personal computer division to Chinese based Lenovo in 2004.

Strengthening System Properties

There are times when disrupting the properties of the opponent's system is impossible, too expensive, or fraught with excessive risk. An alternative strategy is to strengthen the part of the system that benefits you. In these cases, strategists should look for ways to build up their organization's position in the system in an attempt to counterbalance the opponent's leverage. Rather than attenuating the opponent's linkages to the system, the idea is to strengthen your links to the system by fortifying some of the system's properties.

Procter and Gamble (P&G) entered the Russian market in 1991, earlier than most of its global and regional competitors, which meant viable nationwide channels of distribution had not yet been established in the country. With the demise of the Soviet Union in December of that year came the collapse of the archaic, government-controlled distribution and logistics infrastructure in the country. While private distribution infrastructure was starting to be built in major urban centers, such as Moscow and St. Petersburg, the rural areas of Russia lagged behind considerably.

The real challenge for the company was how to turn its first mover strategy for Russia into an advantage. While P&G had a global brand that it believed would give it a competitive edge in Russia, the company also knew that it would soon face formidable global and European competitors who would try to enter the market on P&G's coattails.

The company concluded that the traditional approach to emerging markets—launching in major cities and later backfilling into the rural hinterlands—wouldn't give it the sustainable competitive advantages it needed. P&G believed that by focusing only on Moscow and St. Petersburg, where emerging private distribution channels were lowering any real entry barriers to the competition, it could lose its first-mover advantage very quickly. But the company also saw a strategic opportunity for trumping the competition, despite these challenges. Their analysis showed that in contrast to the major cities, where the competition would likely heat up quickly, there were huge swaths of unmet demand in Russia's rural areas. Moreover, in these areas, distribution and logistics networks were either weak or non-existent. Whereas the competition could use the existing distribution and logistics networks to pick the low-hanging fruit of the urban markets, they would be blocked from entering the rural markets because of the lack of viable distribution channels.

P&G saw that if it could somehow figure a way around the distribution problems in the rural areas, it could unlock new demand for its products and create a barrier that competition would find difficult, if not impossible, to surmount. Instead of attacking competition in the urban markets, P&G focused its strategy at the system level, building distribution infrastructure that enabled it to tap into the demand in the rural markets. By shaping an industry structure fraught with competitive challenges, instead of adapting to it, P&G was able to gain the competitive advantage.

While the company didn't physically build its own distribution centers in the rural areas, it did form partnerships with local distributors to build capacity in the marketplace. On their own, these distributors were inadequate and underpowered to penetrate the market, but P&G focused on building them up and making them a potent market force. On behalf of this strategy, P&G provided working capital to thirty-two handpicked distributors, arming them with state-of-the art information technology and providing them with delivery vans. The result was world-class distributors that could sell and service local supermarkets and retailers. In return, these distributors agreed to remain exclusive to P&G, effectively shutting out the competition.

Procter and Gamble built the distribution function into the industry to offset the low entry barriers that benefited competition in the urban markets. Aside from winning by gaining the rural markets, this strategy gave P&G a beachhead in the rural markets from it could then attack the urban markets.[24]

Creating a New System

Sometimes there is a fine line between strengthening properties of an existing system, such as P&G did, and actually creating a new system. Sometimes tweaking the properties of a system can inadvertently cause it to transform into a completely different system. Introducing disruptive change into a system is risky and can lead to unintended consequences. There are situations, however, where introducing revolutionary change into a system is intentional. Generally these strategies come about as a result of a belief that tweaking an existing system won't improve one's competitive advantage. They are built on an assumption that the new system will be more favorable than the existing system.

One way to create a new system is to tinker with the boundaries of existing systems. As previously discussed, systems have boundaries. The fact that these boundaries comprise the relationships and processes we recognize as part of an interrelated system make even informal boundaries real and meaningful. But meaningful shouldn't be confused with permanent. The landscape is littered with countries and industries whose boundaries changed despite an illusion of permanence.

The following are two examples of how disrupting the boundaries of existing systems can unleash revolutionary change that spawns completely new systems. In the 1950s and 1960s Egypt's then president Gamal Abdel Nasser's strategy was to build a new pan-Arab system on top of the individual state boundaries that were the legacy of the European colonial period. Nasser had come to power as a result of a Free Officers' revolt in 1952, which signaled the beginning of the end of British colonialism in Egypt. He also witnessed other Arab countries enduring a similarly painful process when shedding their colonial yokes. Nasser's strategic insight was that the only way to resist possible European revanchist ambitions, liberate Palestine from Israel, and successfully deal with the ambitions of the superpowers was to mobilize a new ideologically and politically integrated Arab system. So he built a new system by changing the political horizon and boundaries of the existing system.

The mantra that accompanied Nasser's strategy was "strength through unity," and he pressed forward, creating an Arab agenda that would be advanced through an Arab political system. He believed the new integrated system would be able to generate more power and leverage against enemies than the old artificial boundaries. He did several things as part of his strategy. First, he mobilized the Arab masses on behalf of a pan-Arab, as opposed to individual country identities, and he wrapped this Arab identity around a core agenda of non-alignment and the liberation of Palestine. He was able to motivate populaces across the Arab world in ways that other leaders in the region couldn't. Second, he worked to forge political unity between individual states, which culminated in an actual merger between Egypt and Syria in 1958. The creation of the United Arab Republic—which converted an informal system composed of independent Arab countries into a formal Arab union comprising two independent states (Egypt and Syria)—was an attempt to create a new system by widening the boundaries of the old. While the union came to an untimely end in 1961, it demonstrated the extent to which Nasser would go to collapse the boundaries of the existing political system on behalf of creating a new one. Finally, he verbally attacked Arab leaders, like King Hussein of Jordan, whom he saw as lackeys of the west and impediments to progress.

Nasser's Arab nationalist bravado led him to a reckless confrontation with Israel in 1967, which brought a humiliating defeat for his Arab experiment. Ultimately Nasser's strategy of collapsing boundaries failed to generate Arab unity and independence. Nevertheless, Nasser's attempt to create a new system that could be used to generate leverage over regional actors and international actors was partially successful. It created local and regional support, as well as created significant leverage over the United States and Britain, although this leverage was squandered in the reckless acts of 1967.

Now let's look at how a business can create a new industry system by disrupting the current boundaries.[25] Apple Computer initially operated within the boundaries of the personal computer industry, but by the early 1990s their strategies within the PC industry were running out of steam, and the company was facing the possibility of insolvency. Then, in 1997, Steve Jobs returned to Apple. He redefined the company, rejuvenated and added to its product lines, and pushed out beyond the confining boundaries of the PC industry. While he introduced some new innovative computer products, like the iMac, his first blockbuster product was the iPod along with the much-vaunted iTunes software.

With this one bold and innovative new product, Jobs disrupted the boundaries separating the computer and media industries. The iPod was a media product, but it operated in tandem with iTunes, which required a personal computer. Apple was now competing in both the computer and music and entertainment industries, not wholly residing in either, but pushed up against the boundaries of both.

It was Apple's next blockbuster product, the iPhone, and later the iPad, which actually caused industry boundaries to collapse and reform as the new mobile computing industry. While Apple's was not the first smartphone, its entry had the greatest disruptive impact. Prior to the launch of the iPhone, the boundaries between the telephone, computer, camera, and music industries were clearly delineated and discrete. Each industry operated according to its own logic, economics, and distribution channels, and there was little overlap between them. Apple's iPhone created convergence and smashed these boundaries.

Did the collapse of industry boundaries and the creation of a new industry affect Apple's competitive position? It immediately gave Apple competitive advantage over its traditional competitors like Dell who weren't innovating fast enough. Consumers flocked to Apple because of its innovative product features and its edgy design. The real competitive advantages came over companies with which Apple had never competed before like Nokia, Samsung, and Motorola. These cell phone companies were not prepared for Apple's foray into their markets, because even though they were aware of Apple's impending product launch, they tended to be dismissive of the threat posed by the iPhone. They were then blindsided by Apple's incredible success. The iPhone was a truly revolutionary product, offering features and designs, as well as access to an unrivaled iTunes ecosystem of app providers, that couldn't be matched by Nokia or Motorola. While Nokia and others had been at the top of the market, they were now relegated to the unenviable middle market position. By disrupting industry boundaries, Apple pushed Nokia and Motorola from their perches as market leaders, taking that position for itself.[26]

What we have covered in this section are ways to create competitive advantage by adapting to or shaping the properties of business and political systems. While these indirect strategies may not themselves lead to a decisive victory over the opponent, they can be effective in tilting the leverage balance just enough to make a direct strategy against the opponent more effective and successful.

Strategies Aimed at the Opponent's Position within the System

Up to this point we have looked at disrupting an opponent's ties to its external system environment. We have examined strategies for interrupting an opponent's relationships within the system and as well as the properties of the system that benefit it. However, leverage can also be created by how an opponent is physically positioned within the system. North Korea, for example, derives a certain amount of leverage over

China because of its position as a buffer state; it separates China from U.S.-backed South Korea. Because China shudders at the thought of a Western-leaning, reunified Korea on its border, it is tolerant of certain behaviors from the government in Pyongyang. Because of its geopolitical position as a buffer state, North Korea's leverage over China is disproportionate to its size and power.

How can one attack something as unassailable as a physical position? One of the main ways is to counteract the effect of the opponent's position through direct engagement and even confrontation. While the opponent won't lose its advantage of position, direct engagement can influence how the opponent uses the advantages of positioning. These direct strategies will be covered more extensively in chapter 4. But the question addressed in this chapter is whether there are indirect ways to neutralize the positioning advantages of an opponent. In reality, the answer is probably not. But you can try to shift your strategy so that the opponent's positioning advantages can't be used against you. In other words, by partially disengaging, you deny the opponent the ability to leverage its position. While this option may not always be available, partial disengagement can sometimes paradoxically improve one's leverage position.

Let's use the U.S.-Iran case to highlight this. Part of Iran's leverage vis-à-vis the United States comes from its geopolitical position in the Persian Gulf. If Iran were attacked, it could retaliate against the United States by disrupting shipping through the Strait of Hormuz, one of the busiest and most critical waterways for the flow of oil to the west. This would drive up oil prices, potentially pushing the U.S. and even world economy back into recession.

But what can be done to reduce the leverage Iran enjoys over the United States due to its geopolitical positioning? Communicating clearly that the United States would act decisively against any attempt on the part of Iran to block the Strait of Hormuz is one way to influence Iran's behavior. But the United States could also gradually shift its long-term strategy away from Iran's positioning advantages. One way is to find alternatives to oil and gas from the Persian Gulf. The support the United States has given to several alternative domestic and international oil sources is an attempt to do just this. Support for the Baku Tbilisi Ceyhan (BTC) pipeline project, which takes oil from the Caspian Sea through Azerbaijan, Georgia, and Turkey and then on to Western markets, is part of a strategy of reducing dependence on oil from the volatile Persian Gulf area.[27] This, combined with other oil and gas pipeline projects and oil drilling off the U.S. gulf coast, is designed to reduce the amount of oil imported to the United States from the Middle East. So, while the United States can't dethrone Iran from its position in the Persian Gulf, it can, over time, reduce the leverage Iran enjoys from that position. While neither perfect nor quick, a strategic shift can be a way to move outside the zone of vulnerability of an opponent's positioning advantages.

CONCLUSION

Strategy within the dimension of systems is important because winning against an adversary requires both the creation and exploitation of leverage. While leverage of an opponent can come from its own internal capability, it can also come from its linkages with the outside world. Strategy in the dimension of systems is designed to subtract the leverage the opponent receives from the outside world. These strategies aim to disrupt relationships the opponent has in its external environment, neutralize benefits it receives from the properties of this external environment, and try to offset the beneficial effects it gets from its position within the environment. While indirect system strategies may not always be sufficient, they are necessary. They can help create competitive advantage when direct confrontation is too risky or ill advised, and they can help tilt the leverage seesaw in your direction, increasing the likelihood that any direct confrontation with opponent will end successfully for you.

4 STRATEGY IN THE DIMENSION OF OPPONENTS

Up to this point our discussion of strategy has not focused on the opponent itself, but rather on ways to influence the opponent's external environment. In other words, the emphasis has been on indirect as opposed to direct strategies. However, as important and necessary as indirect strategies are, they are normally insufficient. While strategy in the dimension of systems plays an important role in compromising the leverage of the opponent, it doesn't necessarily obviate the need for direct engagement.

Strategy against the opponent is very distinct from systems strategy. While strategy in the systems environment is analogous to a game of billiards, where the goal of pocketing one ball is achieved by hitting another ball, strategy against opponents is similar to fencing, where winning involves maneuvering to either defeat an adversary or disrupt its plans.[1] Strategy in the dimension of systems tends to be highly complex and abstract, but strategy against the opponent tends to be more concrete and easier to conceptualize. Think of strategy in the dimension of systems as focusing on the forest, while strategy at the level of the opponent focuses more granularly on the trees. Lastly, direct strategy against an opponent tends to entail higher risk than indirect strategies in the system. While strategies at the systems level may fly beneath the opponent's radar and not provoke a retaliatory response, strategies against an opponent have a higher probability of eliciting a strong reaction.

STRATEGIC ANALYSIS OF OPPONENTS

Although strategic analysis in the dimension of the opponent is concrete, it has its own set of challenges. Difficult judgment calls need to be made that defy the use of any boiler-plate methods. Doing systematic analysis of a particular opponent may be somewhat easier than analyzing the broader systems environment, but it still involves as much art as science. Moreover, the stakes involved with this type of analysis are extremely high, as an incorrect reading of the capabilities and motives of an opponent can lead to failed strategy or even complete defeat.

One of the most difficult judgments to make in this analysis involves identification of the opponent. While it may be clear who the opponent is in situations of all-out conflict between countries or companies, in other circumstances the opponent may be less clear. In today's complex international system, it's not always clear who should be considered an opponent of the United States. Should China be considered an opponent? Does Iran make the cut, or is it more of a regional nemesis than a real threat to the security of the country. Is Pakistan an ally or an opponent? In a post–Osama bin Laden world, al-Qaeda constitutes a threat, but to what degree? Deciding who makes it onto the threat radar screen is critical, but not always clear.

Deciding who an opponent is can be difficult even in theater-specific situations. Is the Taliban the only opponent to U.S. efforts in Afghanistan that should be put under the analytic microscope? Or should some of the warlords and fundamentalist militant groups like Hezb-e-Islami also be included? And to complicate matters further, how should the analyst discern between the various Taliban factions in Afghanistan, and their Pakistani Taliban counterparts? These are the types of critical decisions that need to be made before drilling down into the analysis of any particular opponent.

The same ambiguities and difficulties apply to businesses trying to decide which competitors to set their sights on. In some situations it may be completely clear who the competitor is. Take for instance the case of Nokia in the cell phone market. In 2007 there was little doubt that Motorola and Samsung were competitors to Nokia. But as we saw in the previous chapter, the iPhone was well on its way to becoming a blockbuster product before Nokia actually saw Apple as a formidable competitive threat.[2]

So how should the strategist identify the opponent in ambiguous situations? Who has both the capability and the motivation to prevent you from reaching your goals? Strategists need to watch for potential opponents who might not pose an immediate threat, but have the capacity, and potentially the will, to eventually interrupt their strategy. One could argue that had Nokia and Motorola looked beyond their immediate cast of competitors to those who had both the means and the will to threaten their market position, Apple would have made it onto their radar screens.

Once an opponent has been identified, what kind of further analysis is necessary before coming up with strategies? An analysis of an actual or potential opponent should include three basic elements. It should consist of an assessment of the opponent's capability, motivation, and strategy. Evaluating capability indicates whether an opponent has the option to interfere with your goals and strategy. Capability won't tell you whether the opponent will actually try to disrupt your strategy, but it does give a window onto what its range of possibilities are. The strategist also needs to know something about the opponent's motivation. Assuming the opponent has the capability to interfere with your strategy, what would be its reason for doing so? Finally, the strategist needs to understand something about the opponent's strategy.[3] Analyzing the opponent's strategy and plans for executing it will be critical to developing a counter-strategy.

Looking at the opponent through these three lenses provides an essential foundation upon which to develop a strategy. Strategy in this dimension can work through the mechanisms of crimping the opponent's capability, thereby narrowing its range of options; shaping its motivation, thereby influencing how it decides among competing options; or disrupting its strategy, thereby interfering with its actions or limiting their effect on you.

Analyzing the Opponent's Capability

Analyzing the capability of the opponent has some unique challenges that aren't encountered in an assessment of one's own capability. One is that estimates of an opponent's capability may be based on unverified, unofficial, and sometimes imperfect data. Sometimes intelligence on an opponent's capability is available, but it can also be unreliable. A good example is the faulty intelligence on the presence of weapons of mass destruction (WMD) in Iraq in the lead-up to the U.S. invasion in 2003. Another challenge can be the adversary's willful attempts to dissemble.

This can be true of a country that uses bravado to embellish its military capability to deter an enemy, or a business that creates smokescreens about its financial or marketing capability to scare off would be competitors. Last, it is difficult to estimate future capability solely on the basis of the opponent's current capability. As we saw in chapter 2 strategy involves manufacturing capability out of a repertoire of resources. Although strategic resources may be fixed, they can be reconfigured on the fly to make a new set of expansive capabilities. Without reliable intelligence and analysis, it is difficult to predict what future capability the opponent could forge out of existing resources.

Keeping these caveats in mind, there are three different questions the strategist needs to address in order to get a fix on the capability of an opponent. The first is, what is the breadth of the opponent's capabilities? In other words, how many different capabilities are in the opponent's portfolio? This involves identifying each of the capabilities the opponent could marshal to challenge you.

A follow-on question is, which of the capabilities serves as the linchpin that holds the system together and if neutralized would render all other capabilities ineffective? Identifying the linchpin is important to gain an understanding not only of the opponent's strength but also its Achilles' heel.

The second question is what is the range of these capabilities? Determining this involves estimating how far the opponent's capability can be projected. For example, is the adversary capable of projecting military, economic, or political power globally, or just regionally? Does it only have the capacity to defend itself against an attack, or could it also retaliate or even launch an offensive?

The third question is how sustainable are these capabilities. This is of particular significance when capabilities are backed by hard, tangible resources that get expended during the execution of the strategy. A company trying to overwhelm a competitor would try to estimate how long the competitor's financial capability would sustain a possible price war. Sustainability can also be relevant when intangibles like political will and resolve are important contributors to capability. The North Atlantic Treaty Organization (NATO), for example, would likely have made some estimates as to how long the political will in the member countries could be sustained in the campaign against the Qaddafi regime in Libya in 2011. How long a capability can be sustained in the midst of battle is a critical question for any strategist.

The following are a few national security and business examples of how the strategist might analyze an opponent's capability. Here is a look at Iran's portfolio of capabilities through the lens of a U.S. policymaker. If the United States' goal is to prevent Iran from developing a nuclear weapon, the analysis needs to identify Iran's existing and potential capabilities to prevent that goal. Before identifying specific capabilities, however, it is important to ask what strategy Iran is likely to use to prevent the United States from achieving its goal. It is within the context of this strategy that we can better understand the capabilities Iran may marshal.

There are a couple different strategic paths Iran could pursue. One would be to preempt the United States by racing toward a nuclear weapons rapid breakout capability before an effective counterstrategy could be marshaled. A breakout capability would provide the capacity to build a nuclear weapon in short order, but stop short of actually producing the weapon. The assumption is that once the United States faces the fait accompli of Iran having a breakout capability, its bargaining position would have been compromised. The second strategy Iran could pursue is to build a credible system of deterrence, by making the risk of a military strike on its nuclear facilities unacceptably high for the United States and Israel. It could threaten to retaliate against U.S. interests in Iraq, in Lebanon through its proxy Hezbollah, and in the economically critical Persian Gulf, if Israel or the United States mounted an attack on its nuclear installation. The third path would be for Iran to hunker down and withstand the withering punitive sanctions against it while continuing to enrich uranium beyond the 20 percent level needed for weapons grade material. The assumption here is that while Iran is hunkering down, it will be able to use delay tactics to forestall a military attack. None of these paths are mutually exclusive and in fact can be mutually reinforcing.

So if these are Iran's possible scenarios for challenging the United States, what capabilities does it have or could build on the fly to make these strategies viable? Let's look at the first strategy where Iran develops a breakout capability before the United States is able to ratchet up sanctions or marshal a military response.[4] Iran would need the technological capability to push uranium enrichment beyond the 20 percent level and toward the 90 percent plus level needed for weapons grade material.

Moreover, Iran needs diplomatic capability to build opposition in the United Nations and other international forums to using military means to resolve the conflict. Iran's diplomatic and commercial ties with Russia and China seem to indicate that it already has this capability. Iran's importance as a source for oil for China and its economic attractiveness to Russia make it easier for Iran to use its diplomatic capability to dissuade these two countries from joining the United States in any multilateral effort to sanction or strong-arm the country.

Iran's second strategy would be to build a system of deterrence against an attack by the United States. While Iran probably lacks the capacity to repel or protect itself from an attack, it is not bereft of retaliatory capabilities. Iran has a strong missile defense capability, a mining capability, and naval swarming capability, all of which contribute to its ability to retaliate. The missile defense capabilities give Iran the ability to inflict consequences on U.S. forces and its allies. Its mining and naval swarming capabilities could interrupt shipping through the vital arteries of the Strait of Hormuz, which could wreak havoc on the global economy.[5] Iran has also a second line of retaliation and deterrence, made possible by an alliance capability, which includes alliances with both state and non-state actors in the region. Iran's relationships with Syria, Hezbollah, and Islamic jihad give it the ability to project power into the Mediterranean, where the United States and Israel have vital interests. The possibility that an attack on Iran could be met by retaliatory responses from Hezbollah, and possibly Islamic jihad, would have to be factored into any analysis. These two lines of retaliation and deterrence could be quite formidable and have the capacity to elevate the risks of an attack on Iran for the United States and Israel.

The strategist should also ask what the range and sustainability of Iran's retaliatory capabilities are. The Iranians have tried to create the specter of a wide-ranging capability, even if the reality of that capability's range is less. In reality it will depend on the degree Hezbollah is willing to take on risk to support Iran. It is also questionable whether Iran could sustain many rounds of a retaliatory response in the midst of battle. Any retaliatory strike launched by Iran would likely be met with a strong counterattack from the United States or Israel, which would possibly eliminate Iran's capability for further retaliation.

Now let's look at the capabilities that could enable Iran's third strategy—to withstand punishing economic sanctions and to continue to buy time as it proceeds down the nuclear path. Though Iran's economy suffered under the weight of U.S.-led sanctions since they were inaugurated, the country developed new capabilities for dealing with these contingencies. It developed stronger economic ties with Dubai, United Arab Emirates, which acted as a valve for circumventing some of the embargoes on Western goods. But with a crescendo of new sanctions, the devaluation of its currency and the European Union's 2012 ban on importing Iranian oil, it is unclear how long it can sustain this strategy. A critical question for U.S. policymakers is whether Iran has a linchpin capability, because they not only need to identify Iran's source of strength, but also its vulnerability. In this case the linchpin would be the most critical capability that enables Iran to rebuff U.S. efforts on the nuclear issue. In this situation, Iran's retaliatory capability would likely be the linchpin. The uncertainty of what Iran and its regional allies might do if attacked, and the political and economic consequences of these actions, might deter the United States from taking military action. However, if Iran's linchpin retaliatory capability is compromised, perhaps by a collapse of the Assad regime in Syria, its other economic and diplomatic capabilities may not be sufficient to deter the United States or Israel from taking a more hostile and aggressive stance.

Now let's explore how a business might analyze the capability of a competitor. We are working for Apple and charged with doing a capability analysis of the company's competitors in 2007, just as it is getting ready to launch the first iPhone. We'll presume that the company's goal is to garner 39 percent of smartphone industry profits by 2010. How would we assess the competition in terms of its capability to prevent Apple from achieving its goal? More specifically, how would Apple analyze Nokia's capability?

The first question is what possible strategies could Nokia pursue to try to block Apple from achieving its market share goals? One would be to use its leverage with AT&T, Sprint, and Verizon to try to prevent Apple from signing on with any of these major network providers. Although Apple could sell its phones through its own stores, it also needed a network alliance partner to provide cell phone service.[6] Another strategic approach would be for Nokia to try to preempt Apple's new product launch by introducing its own smartphone.

What capabilities could Nokia marshal to block Apple's entry into the cell phone business? It would need to have the market strength, both with its network providers and with its customers, to shut Apple out, or at least slow it down. However, we will never know whether Nokia had the capability to apply pressure to the network providers because Nokia underestimated the threat from Apple and never tried.[7]

What capabilities could Nokia have marshaled to try to stymie Apple's plans by beating them in the marketplace with a better product? Apple would certainly have to factor in to its analysis that Nokia had a technological capability to develop a phone with many of the same features as the iPhone. While lacking the creative design prowess of Apple, Nokia certainly had the technological know-how to build a competitive phone. Nokia also had significant brand power, arguably its linchpin capability, which would have allowed it to aggressively market its product. At the time, Nokia was the leader in the cell phone industry, and had developed incredible market penetration and brand dominance in both developed and emerging markets. Moreover, Nokia had the financial capacity to compete effectively in the smartphone sector had it seen the opportunity early enough. In the end, the problem with Nokia wasn't its lack of capabilities; it was Nokia's lack of will to marshal these capabilities against Apple. However, since Apple wouldn't have known in advance that Nokia's response would be so anemic, they would have had to analyze Nokia's capabilities and assume they would be mobilized to challenge the introduction of the Apple iPhone.

Analyzing the Motivations of the Opponent

While analyzing an opponent's capability reveals its range of available options, it tells us little about how the opponent is likely to prioritize those options and choose among them. An analysis of an opponent's motivation and interests will help narrow down what its preferences and choices might be.

There are several steps involved in analyzing the motivation of an opponent. The first is to infer what the opponent's interests are. The second step is to determine whether the opponent is motivated mostly by threat or opportunity with regard to those. The third step is to ascertain the opponent's tolerance for risk and uncertainty.

Step 1: Analyze the Opponent's Interests

Identifying an opponent's interests is critical in figuring out what it has at stake in any confrontation or engagement. It is important to make a distinction between the opponent's core and situational interests. Core interests are what the opponent needs to protect, create, or promote in order to ensure its overall well-being. For countries there are some common core national interests such as security, economic vitality, and sovereignty. Countries also have unique core interests, which are specific to their own particular circumstances. Israel, for example, has a critical core interest of water security. It is unlikely, however, that the United States would put water security at the top of its list. Businesses also have unique core interests, as well as some universal core interests such as profitability, sustainability, and shareholder return. Pharmaceutical giants like Pfizer, which rely heavily on patents, will likely view intellectual property protection as a core interest, while for firms in other sectors this would be of a lesser concern.

Situational interests, while derived from core interests, are distinct. Core interests are broader and more enduring, while situational interests tend to be more transitory. Situational interests are specific to what the opponent has at stake in a particular engagement or confrontation. They are what your opponent gains or loses in that particular situation.

It is not unusual for there to be debates over what an opponent's core or situational interests are. While there is no foolproof way for the strategist to discern an opponent's interests, there are some places to look for evidence that can reduce the uncertainty. The first question is whether there are any objective interests that can be inferred. As related before, we can infer that a pharmaceutical company like Pfizer, dependent on patents, will see the emergence of a global intellectual property regime as a core interest. We can also infer that a core interest of a large industry-dominant firm like Microsoft will be the preservation of market share. No intelligence, documents, or deep analysis are required to conclude these are core interests.

But as helpful as objective interests are, they only reveal part of the picture. Leaders interpret the core and situational interests of their countries or businesses in ways that often defy objectivity. That is why it is important to factor what leaders say about their interests and what actions they take into any analysis. Verbal pronouncements by leaders are an important data point, but since they may be politically motivated or be mere bravado, words alone should not be accepted as prima facie evidence of an interest. In addition, the analyst should also look at actions, which are typically a better indication of what the leader believes is important. If the leader identifies something as important and backs words up with action, then the analyst can be reasonably sure that there is an authentic interest at stake. Verbal expressions and actions taken together are the best window onto how leaders view the interests of their organizations.

Step 2: Determine the Opponent's Perception of Threat or Opportunity

After discerning the opponent's interests, the next step is to evaluate whether the opponent perceives mostly threat or opportunity to those interests. This is important in indicating to the strategist what is motivating the opponent. Like much of the analytic work related to strategy, ascertaining whether an opponent operates from a perception of threat or opportunity is neither easy nor straightforward. It involves inferring from the opponent's objective circumstances as well as from what it says and what it does. To further complicate matters, perceptions of threat and opportunity are often comingled.

Putting ourselves in the professional shoes of a U.S. policymaker responsible for evaluating Iran's perceptions of threat and opportunity is instructive. There is evidence to support the view that Iran's actions on the nuclear issue are animated by a combination of threat and opportunity. The most difficult question for the policymaker is which serves as the overriding factor in shaping Iran's behavior. The reality is that when threat and opportunity are both operative, which one has primacy will generally depend on the conflict dynamics at the time.

Let's look at Iran's security environment to see how its leaders might analyze threat to the country's, or perhaps even their own, interests. Looking at Iran's security environment through the lens of an Iranian decision maker, one would observe that the United States, Russia, Israel, Pakistan, and India, all possess a nuclear weapon capability, potentially placing a non-nuclear Iran at a considerable strategic disadvantage. Moreover, one would not fail to observe that the regime itself feels somewhat vulnerable, given the history of animosity between Washington, D.C., and Tehran going back to the Iranian Revolution of 1979. While the U.S. government under President Obama made some initial positive overtures towards Iran, the overall tenor of the relationship over the past thirty years has been confrontational. Perceptions of threat have been reinforced by a U.S. military presence in the Persian Gulf and troops in Iraq and Afghanistan. Given these circumstances it would not be reckless for a U.S. policymaker to conclude that one motive animating Iran's nuclear program is a need to mitigate these perceived threats.

But it would be wrong for a U.S. policymaker to impute all of Iran's motivations to a perception of threat. While the U.S.-led operations in Afghanistan and Iraq initially heightened Iran's perceived threat, over time Iranian leaders started to balance this with a view that U.S. incursions into the region, and the missteps that ensued, presented opportunities as well. First, Iraq's regime, along with its megalomaniacal leader, Saddam Hussein, collapsed in the wake of the U.S. invasion. Having been Iran's nemesis from before the Islamic revolution, a weakened Iraq after the invasion removed a significant source of threat and concern for Iran. Moreover, this provided Iran with greater opportunities to project its influence into Iraq through alliances with several Shi'i parties. In combination with its relationship with Syria, this newfound influence into Iraq also facilitated Iran's ability to project power into the Mediterranean. Additionally, the perception in Tehran was that the U.S. regional position was weakening over time by the brush with civil war in Iraq, and the resurgence of the Taliban in Afghanistan. This meant that Iran's bargaining strength had improved over time, and that with a besieged United States and a weakened Iraq, there were opportunities for Iran to enhance its overall regional position and influence.[8]

So the picture of Iran being animated by threat or opportunity is nuanced and mixed. The circumstances at the time will shape which is the primary motivating factor, something that would have to be followed by a U.S. policymaker. The economic sanctions and the specter of a possible military action are designed to play to Iran's threat perceptions as way to make it more pliant. Whether or not Iran has internalized this and is animated more by threat than opportunity will be revealed by the actions its leadership takes in the negotiations with the West on the nuclear issue.

Step 3: Analyze the Opponent's Tolerance for Risk

The last step in analyzing your opponent's motivation is to estimate their tolerance for risk. This is important as it will provide another data point for the opponent's threshold for action. A risk-averse opponent will likely have a much higher threshold for reacting to an intensely perceived threat to its interests than a more risk-prone opponent. Shying away from the possible harmful consequences, risk-averse opponents are likely to refrain from action unless there is an extremely high perception of threat or opportunity. But the risk-prone opponent is more likely to perceive even a modest sleight to its interests as a provocation deserving of a response, fully understanding that any response could potentially lead to unintended consequences.

The main method for assessing the risk tolerance of an opponent is to track the pattern of its actions over time, and observe the decision-making style of its leaders. Again, while verbal pronouncements shouldn't be disregarded, and in fact can be an important data point, what matters most in calculating risk tolerance is the pattern of actions.

The following is an example of how a policymaker might analyze the decision-making pattern of a leader in order to get a fix on their risk tolerance. Iraq's former president Saddam Hussein was the ultimate practitioner of brinkmanship, whose actions pointed to a high tolerance, or one might argue an appetite, for risk. His pattern of decisions is instructive. Motivated by a desire to settle old scores with Iran, a country he believed to be vulnerable and preoccupied with internal power consolidation following the Islamic Revolution, he launched an invasion of Iran in 1980. While Saddam may have believed that Iran was weaker than it had ever been before, his military invasion nevertheless involved significant risk. Iran fought back harder, longer, and fared better than Saddam ever expected. His actions showed that he had a high tolerance for risk, and was willing to accept the possibility of unintended consequences, when presented with what he saw as an opportunity.

Given this earlier pattern with Iran, U.S. policymakers charged with responding to Saddam's aggression against Kuwait in 1990 shouldn't have been shocked by his reaction to U.S. and UN ultimatums to withdraw his troops. Even under the threat of attack, Saddam elected to dig in his heels. This prompted the United States and its allies to launch Operation Desert Shield, followed by Operation Desert Storm in a successful bid to liberate Kuwait.

Ultimately Saddam's tendency to take wild risks cost him both his regime and his life, when he toyed with the United States over the issue of weapons of mass destruction in 2003. In what appeared to be more of a death wish than a risk calculation, Saddam's rebuff of all demands from the United States led to the U.S. invasion and his eventual downfall. Given his invasion of Iran in 1980 and Kuwait in 1990, policymakers in 2003 had pretty reliable evidence of what Saddam was likely to do when threatened. His proclivity toward risk in the past should have indicated to policymakers that he was unlikely to stand down, even when faced with the prospect of an invasion.

In sum, as imperfect and difficult as it may be to analyze the motivations of an opponent, there are methods and steps to be followed. While the evidence is often ambiguous and even contradictory, there are ways to generate insights by breaking the analysis of motivation down into bite-sized morsels. The first is to tease out what the interests of the opponent are. While not all leaders act in accordance to their objective interests, understanding something about how they interpret interests gets to the core of what motivates them to action or inaction. The second is to gain an understanding of whether the opponent is motivated primarily by perceptions of threat or opportunity. This will help the analyst understand how the opponent is likely to respond to hostile and friendly actions from others. And the third is to assess the risk tolerance of the opponent. This will give insights as to what the threshold for action might be. Taken together, answers to these questions will help strategists project how the opponent is likely to weigh and prioritize the various options it might have. These questions will also help with an understanding of how the opponent is likely to work through the tradeoffs of each of the possible options it might have.

Analyzing the Strategy of the Opponent
In addition to understanding what the opponent is capable of, and what motivates it to act, it is important to understand its strategy. The reason this is important is that a big part of strategy against an opponent involves developing ways to neutralize or disrupt the opponent's strategy.

There are essentially two methods for getting a fix on the opponent's strategy. The first is to look at the public pronouncements of the opponent. Sometimes the strategy itself, or at least hints of the strategy, can be gleaned from what the opponent says publicly, or in some cases, privately. While it is unlikely that a leader of a country or a corporation will telegraph his or her entire plan, the general outline of the strategy can often be gleaned from what is said publically. The United States publically lays out the basic tenets of its national security strategy every couple of years. While the national security strategy doesn't lay bare a road map that could be used against the United States by an enemy, it does articulate priorities and the general outline of strategic imperatives. Businesses, too, in their annual reports generally give enough of the broad outlines of their strategies to satisfy investors, while being careful not to reveal things that could be exploited by competitors. Privately held companies and less democratic countries will keep their strategies more opaque, but even in these cases, following what leaders say about their governments or businesses can be useful.

In situations where very little can be gleaned from verbal pronouncements, or in situations where the strategist believes verbal pronouncements give only a partial picture, it will also be important to look for patterns of behavior from which a strategy can possibly be inferred. Here the strategist will, in a jigsaw puzzle like manner, attempt to infer the opponent's overall strategy from individual snippets of actions.

Here's an example of a national security case. Although the regime of Syrian president Bashar Assad has not publicly articulated its strategy for coping with the uprisings that first erupted in 2011, one can infer it from their pattern of actions. His regime waged a two-prong strategy—a war of words and the use of extreme force. Assad initially used promises of conciliation and flexibility to try to manage the expectations of the protesters, while at the same time delegitimizing their motives by claiming they were terrorists and agents of foreign powers. Since then his words have mostly been aimed at delegitimizing the rebels, as it is probably too late for any real conciliation. His strategy of using extreme force was designed to prevent the rebels from gaining any sustainable momentum by breaking their will and the will of communities that might be supportive of the anti-government cause. The violent part of his strategy, which seems to have been taken out of Iran's playbook for suppressing the protests by the Green Movement in 2009, seems to be faltering.

On the business side, Apple Inc. seldom speaks publicly about its strategy, but there are ways to infer the company's strategy from its decisions and actions. The key is looking at the new product rollouts over several years and seeing that the company follows a platform strategy—

all of its products are built with similar technologies, software and user interfaces, and integrate together. The iPhone, iPod, and iPad are all examples of this type of strategy. Moreover, product features and software that are successful in one product are quickly rolled out out to the others. While Apple seldom discusses this, the analyst and competitor can glean this pattern from the decisions that have been made and actions that have been taken.

But inferring a strategy from actions alone can sometimes involve considerable risk. In many cases the pattern of actions will be inconsistent, ambiguous, and point to a couple of possible strategic paths. Moreover, despite what may appear to be a pattern of behavior, there may actually be no underlying coherent strategy. Imputing individual actions to a broad strategy when none exists can lead to the wrong conclusions. The evidence used to attribute a strategy to Saddam Hussein before the 2003 Iraq war is a case in point. The Bush administration inferred from his actions and statements a strategy involving weapons of mass destruction that wasn't real. This example points out another risk, which is that tracking past actions might lead a analyst to believe that a strategy that has already been abandoned is still operational. In Iraq, when U.S. policymakers assumed that a past pattern of accumulating weapons of mass destruction and using them against the Kurds in Iraq was indicative of a current strategy, they were wrong. Rather than revealing a strategy, Saddam Hussein's words and actions proved to be a cover of bravado to conceal the fact that there was no strategy.

STRATEGY IN THE DIMENSION OF OPPONENTS

Influencing the behavior of an opponent is one of the most difficult things a strategist must do. While there is no silver bullet formula for this, there are a few different mechanisms that the strategist should be considering when faced with an opponent's challenge. The strategist should use the analysis discussed in the first half of this chapter as the canvas for looking for strategic options. The first option is to attenuate, and in some cases neutralize, the opponent's capability. The second involves altering the opponent's motivations and intentions. The third mechanism involves disrupting the opponent's strategy, or at least the effectiveness of that strategy.[9]

These three different mechanisms shouldn't be viewed as mutually exclusive, but rather as complementary. Oftentimes strategies will draw from all three to influence or counter the behavior of the opponent, as the United States did in its "shock and awe" strategy in the 2003 invasion of Iraq. The bombing raids neutralized the capability of the Iraqi military and the Republican Guard, but were also intended to demoralize the regime and reduce its motivation to fight, as well as to disrupt the strategy of the regime. The mutually reinforcing mechanisms quickly led to the collapse of Saddam Hussein's regime.

Targeting the Opponent's Capability

The idea behind targeting an opponent's capability is to force it into a position that is sub-optimal for it, but favorable to you. Impairing capability is a critical piece of what it takes to influence the behavior of the opponent, and needs to be a critical part of the strategist's toolbox. Targeting the opponent's capability is, in some ways, an attack on its strategy. Dismantling or attenuating the opponent's capabilities is designed to weaken its strategic muscle, severely limiting its range of motion and ability to act.

Capability has three different dimensions, and the strategist should be thinking about weakening or crippling an opponent's capability across all of them. The strategist should be focused on narrowing the breadth, shortening the range, and limiting the sustainability of the opponent's capability. Neutralizing the opponent's capability across these three critical dimensions offers the potential to constrict and limit its range of motion.

Narrowing the repertoire of capabilities the opponent has at its disposal can occur in a few different ways. One is to identify and then try to neutralize individual capabilities. A company that tries to undermine a competitor might target the competitor's brand power. It may do this by refuting the competitor's claims that it engages in ethical practices in its sourcing of raw materials. It may refute these claims publicly and directly, or it might feed information to a non-profit organization or to an investigative journalist. Whether the claim is legitimate or not, the goal is to erode the competitor's reputation, eat into its brand equity, and deprive it of the capability to use its brand to its benefit. The same company may also target the competitor's financial capability, waging a costly price war in an attempt to drain it of the working capital it needs.

Another way to compromise the opponent is by targeting its linchpin capability, which indirectly targets all other capabilities. Remember that the linchpin is the primary capability upon which all others depend.[10] By targeting the linchpin the strategist weakens the glue that holds the portfolio of capabilities together. Liddell Hart, one of the most esteemed military historians, put it eloquently when he said that "it should be the aim of grand strategy to discover and pierce the Achilles' heel of the opposing government's power to make war. And strategy, in turn, should seek to penetrate a joint in the harness of the opposing forces."[11] That joint in the harness of the opponent is the linchpin capability.

What do we mean by targeting an opponent's linchpin capability? Does it mean launching a physical attack in order to disable a capability? Sometimes the answer can be yes. In this vein, the Israelis and the United States were probably behind the Stuxnet computer worm, which attacked Iran's centrifuges at its nuclear enrichment sites. Israel may have been behind the assassination of several of Iran's top nuclear scientists and has also expressed a willingness to launch a military attack on Iran's uranium enrichment sites should the nuclear program continue.

However, attacking an opponent's capability directly isn't always feasible. The opponent may have clear power advantages or the capability may be immune to attack. In these circumstances, crippling an opponent's capabilities has to happen in other ways. You may need to indirectly target your opponent's capability, or reduce the effect of the opponent's capability rather than disrupting the capability itself. This could be accomplished by building up rival capabilities. Companies, for example, can develop unique and differentiated capabilities that cancel out the effect of the competitor's strengths.[12] Countries can develop asymmetric capabilities, designed to attenuate the effectiveness of the enemy's capabilities. By doing so, you may be able to render the opponent's linchpin capability ineffective by developing a rival capability, which can then turn the opponent's linchpin capability into a liability.

Take for example the battle between online retailer Amazon and bookseller Barnes and Noble. Arguably the linchpin of Barnes and Noble's capability is its real-estate prowess in locating stores in prime retail spots across the country. This capability gave the company a competitive advantage that seemed almost bullet proof.

What strategic possibilities could undermine Barnes and Noble's capability? Before its recent move to start closing locations, one might have tried to rival it by competing head-to-head for new lease space as the chain continued to grow, in an effort to deprive it of prime locations in the future. But with the chain's head start, it would have been unlikely that trying to match its capability tit-for-tat would have been successful. But Barnes and Noble is vulnerable to a competitor that rivals it with a completely different capability. Amazon's strategy of delivering books directly to the consumers' homes at a considerably lower price involved a completely new set of capabilities. Its primary capability was customer management, backed up by its formidable data mining and logistics. It provided an unmatched online experience for the customer, using past purchase history to make suggestions for future purchases. Moreover, it used the introduction of the Kindle e-reader to further distance itself from brick and mortar booksellers. While Barnes and Noble's traditional approach of using the strength of its stores against competitors worked against Borders and other brick-and-mortar booksellers, it didn't work against Amazon. By differentiating its strategy and coming up with different rival capabilities, Amazon turned Barnes and Noble's linchpin capability into a liability. Saddled with brick and mortar stores, it had difficulty responding to the challenge posed by Amazon.[13]

So far we have focused on crippling the opponent by reducing its breadth of capabilities. But the strategist also has to think about ways to reduce the range and sustainability of the opponent's capability. That is, in addition to considering ways to deprive the opponent of certain capabilities, it is also important to consider ways to reduce the extent to which particular capabilities can be projected, as well as how long the capability muscle can remain flexed, without starting to wither.

What follows are different strategic approaches for shortening the range and limiting the sustainability of the opponent's capability. While reducing the breadth of an opponent's capability requires identifying and targeting specific capabilities, the challenges involved in shortening the range and limiting the sustainability of its capabilities are different. Here the purpose is to deprive the opponent of the resources it needs to project and sustain its capability, and to attack the links that connect the different capabilities. In this case, the challenge is more of countering the opponent's overall ability to feed its capabilities, and less of trying to counter the individual capabilities themselves.

Root Attack Strategies

One type of strategic approach for limiting the sustainability and range of the opponent's capabilities involves targeting the roots that nourish them. Capabilities have to be replenished in order to be viable and sustainable in conflict, and this nourishment can be in the form of both tangible and intangible resources. The military capability of a country and the financial capability of a company draw heavily on expendable tangible resources like munitions and capital, respectively. While intangible resources like management and leadership are also critically important, military and financial capabilities will likely collapse if deprived of tangible resources such as equipment and capital. Root attack strategies target the source and flow of the tangible, and sometimes intangible, resources that fuel and sustain capability. Attacking the roots of the opponent's capability chokes off its ability to sustain its operations.

Historically naval blockades have been a method for choking an opponent's capabilities. The Israeli government's naval blockade of Gaza was just such an attempt. It was designed to undermine Hamas' capability by depriving it of the critical resources it needed to sustain its political, military, and economic capabilities. Another way to do this, short of creating a physical barrier like a blockade, is to create a political barrier by convincing the opponent's allies to impose an embargo on valuable resources. What would the effect on Hezbollah's overall capability be if Iran, as part of some grand bargain, agreed to reduce the support it gave to the organization? Even though it would be possible for Hezbollah to find new sources of arms to maintain its military prowess, cutting it off from Syria and Iran would be certainly a blow to its capability.

Companies, too, can use this method of hobbling the capability of a competitor. Consider the case of a market leader in the technology field trying to stop or slow down a new upstart competitor entering the market. One possibility would be to try to deprive the competitor access to a critical component needed to manufacture its product. If the company is dominant enough in its industry, it might try to strong-arm its suppliers, dissuading them from selling critical technology to the new competitor. Another tactic is to buy the company that supplies critical technology, and then cancel or not renew its supply contracts with competitors. Companies that wield power and influence over their supply chains can use root-attack strategies to disadvantage a competitor, depriving it of critical technology and supplies.

Base Attack Strategies

While root attack strategies work to deprive the opponent of the nourishment that fuels its capability, base attack strategies aim to disrupt its operational center. Base attack strategies, which destroy the linkages or glue connecting the system of capabilities, have been part of the discourse on strategy since the classical theorists wrote on the subject. Some classical scholars of strategy like Clausewitz and Antoine-Henri Jomini argued that the capital city is the base, or center of gravity, of an opponent's capability.[14] Although capital cities may not always constitute the base or center of a country's overall capability, the principle of neutralizing, or at least hobbling, an enemy's operational base still holds. Hitting the enemy at the decisive point where all operations and capabilities converge can certainly work to weaken its capability.[15]

The challenge in today's environment is to identify the base of the opponent's capability. A company's strategic base is generally not its operational hub or headquarters, but rather where its market is most concentrated. Companies typically rely on a base of core customers that give it a platform from which to expand into new products and attack new markets. These core customers are probably what constitute the company's base. It could be a cluster of key customers with similar characteristics or a large group of customers whose contribution to revenues and profits is disproportionally large. Sometimes the base is the geographic area where business is concentrated. Undercutting that customer or market base can hurt the competitor by reducing its range of motion and sustainability.

What are some of the specific ways companies can deal a crippling blow to a competitor's capability by attacking its market base? Trying to woo away the company's largest customers is one way. It is not unusual for companies to view the customers who give them the most revenue as covering their fixed costs. These customers may not generate a lot of profit for the company, but they do absorb the overhead costs of the business. Once fixed overhead costs are covered by the revenue flowing from large clients, higher profit margin revenues from the smaller, and generally more numerous, clients lead to the overall profitability of the firm. Without the revenue from these large clients, however, it is unlikely that even a high profit margin from smaller customers will be sufficient to keep a company afloat. So attacking the competitor's largest clients is one way to attack its base, render it unprofitable, and reduce its range and limit its sustainability.

It may appear that base attack strategies are relevant only when facing an opponent with weaker or equal capability. This has some validity since these strategies will almost always prompt a retaliatory move. In other words, a strong actor retaliating against a weaker attacker would more than likely be able to erase any benefits the weaker opponent accrued from the base attack. So how can a smaller or weaker actor launch a base attack strategy where the risk of a counterattack is outweighed by a likelihood of success? Also, how does one attack a base of any opponent, weak or strong, when it is heavily defended?

One strategy that can be effective when direct and immediate attack on the opponent's base may court disaster is what is known as a flanking strategy. A flanking strategy targets areas that are only lightly defended by the opponent, allowing a smaller or weaker party to take advantage of gaps in the larger opponent's defenses. It gives the smaller party an opportunity to burrow its way into a larger opponent, sometimes even escaping detection, while simultaneously building strength for an ultimate frontal assault on the base.

One of the most emblematic examples of a business flanking strategy was used by Wal-Mart in its competition with Kmart. When Wal-Mart first started expanding beyond its base in Rogers, Arkansas, in the 1960s it concentrated its efforts on small rural towns. It didn't really try to compete with the much larger and more powerful Kmart, whose stores tended to be in larger towns and cities with populations greater than 50,000 people. Had Wal-Mart tried to attack Kmart's base market head-on in those early years, it probably would have provoked a strong, and perhaps overwhelming, response. At the time Kmart had incredible market, supplier, brand, and advertising power, which could have been deployed to overwhelm its smaller rival. Instead Wal-Mart built momentum in the undefended areas of the market—the small and medium sized towns—and stayed away from K-Mart's base. But once it built momentum, and a base of its own in the secondary and tertiary markets, Wal-Mart began attacking the larger cities that constituted the base of Kmart's market. By 1993, 82 percent of Kmart's stores faced Wal-Mart as a competitor.[16] So, while it started with a flanking strategy, Wal-Mart ultimately pursued a base attack strategy against Kmart. The flanking strategy allowed a Wal-Mart to enter undefended areas of the market, build strength and momentum, and then later attack Kmart's market base.

Base Denial Strategies

Another way to limit the scope and sustainability of an opponent's capability is to prevent it from establishing a base. The premise is that it is easier to deny than dislodge the enemy from a base. This could be relevant for a company trying to prevent a competitor from successfully establishing a base in a new market or country, or for a military trying to deny the enemy a foothold in a particular piece of territory.

In the early days of the Cold War the United States and Soviet Union each jockeyed for allies. There was a tacit understanding between the two nuclear-armed superpowers that direct confrontation between them would be mutually destructive and therefore unthinkable. This agreement did not translate into a complete abandonment of competition, merely the avoidance of direct confrontation. Instead the superpowers tried to create alliances with the most strategically important countries in each region, forcing the other to settle for the less attractive ally. To the chagrin of the United States, the Soviet Union was effective in getting Egypt to buy arms and seek support from it in the 1950s. In what was viewed as a zero-sum game, the Soviet Union denied the United States a political base in Egypt, the most populous and strategically important country in the Arab world, forcing the United States to align itself with less significant countries like Jordan.

To conclude, targeting the opponent's capability is designed to limit the range of options it has available. Strategies that target capability are designed to severely limit the opponent, forcing it towards options that may be less favorable to them and more favorable to you. The key is to neutralize as many aspects of the opponent's capability as possible. Targeting the opponent's linchpin capability provides an opportunity to cripple the entire breadth of capabilities. There are also specific points that can be targeted that have the potential to limit the range and sustainability of the opponent's capability. Attacking the roots of the opponent's capability can choke it from the resources it needs. Attacking or denying it a base has the potential to cripple the opponent's core, preventing it from taking advantage of the resources it has.

Targeting the Opponent's Motivation

While the previous section addressed strategic moves that try to prevent the opponent from taking particular actions by disrupting its capability, this section will focus on influencing the behavior of the opponent by altering its decision-making calculus. In other words, rather than blocking the opponent from a particular action, the idea is to motivate it to act differently.

Shaping the Opponent's Situational Interests

One way to influence the behavior of an opponent is to shape its interests, which requires looking for ways to alter what the opponent has at stake in a particular situation. The idea behind strategies of this ilk is that by altering what the opponent has to gain or lose in a particular situation, its decisional calculus and ultimately its behavior will be influenced. This is done by forcing the opponent to choose among competing interests.

Typically the leader of a country or business tries to manage the tradeoffs between multiple interests. In the ideal world, the leader has the wherewithal to satisfy all interests, without having to choose one interest over another. Generally conflict erupts when in attempting to satisfy the full range of interests, the opponent challenges yours. It is the job of the strategist through the use of a combination of "carrots" and "sticks" to persuade the opponent that its current or planned course of action will make it impossible for it to fulfill all or most of its critical interests. By bringing sufficient pressure to bear you force your opponent into a corner, making it clear that it can't have all of its interests, and forcing it to make a choice. Moreover, the way you are applying pressure is designed to get the opponent to choose the interest that least conflicts with yours.

A business example will help illustrate how forcing tradeoffs between competing interests can get an opponent to change direction.

Consider a company whose CEO initially rebuffs a competitor's offer to acquire or merge with them but then suddenly becomes more receptive when the competitor imposes severe consequences for doing otherwise. What follows is this scenario. Company A decides to make an offer to buy its competitor, company B. The CEO of company B politely refuses the offer, replying that the management team has no interest in selling the company at this time. Despite efforts to woo company B with a very attractive financial offer, the resistance to company A's entreaties continues. After many conversations between the two parties, it is clear that company B doesn't see it in its interests to sell. In fact, company B clearly states its belief that preserving its independence is preferable to the disruption that would come from a merger. It believes that it can preserve its interests of financial viability and independence by resisting the offer from company A.

Company A is not dissuaded, deciding that buying company B is too critical to its future to drop the issue. So it starts its strategy of forcing company B to choose among competing interests, something it has not done up to this point. Company A targets company B's top ten customers, using all of the pricing and marketing muscle it has to convince them to desert company B and start buying product from company A. Since company A has comparative advantages of a stronger brand and lower manufacturing costs, it undercuts company B's price by 20 percent, successfully wooing away two major customers, which together represent 15 percent of company B's revenues.

The following week the CEO of company A calls up his counterpart at company B, requesting a meeting. When they sit down the CEO of company B berates the CEO of company A for stealing its customers. The CEO of company A calmly warns the CEO of company B that this is just the beginning—either company B agrees to be acquired by company A, or the next eight largest customers will be targeted. The language used by the company A's CEO is that they will either acquire company B at a fair market price, or they will steal the company by winning over its customers.

Ninety days later a transaction was finalized merging company A and company B, giving the CEO of the former exactly what he wanted. By using its market and pricing power, company A forced company B to choose between its interests of financial solvency and independence.

While the financial incentives or "carrots" of the offer weren't sufficient to create tension between these interests, the strategy of attacking company B's position in the marketplace was. By selling to company A, the management team preserved the financial position of the company, even thought it had to sacrifice its independence. If it had continued to resist company A, company B risked losing both its financial position and its independence interests. At least by buckling under the pressure, company B preserved its financial interests.

This scenario focused mostly on using threats or "sticks" to persuade the opponent to alter its behavior. But there are also times when presenting your opponent with an opportunity or "carrot" might influence its behavior. In this case the idea is to use a different and even more compelling set of interests to change what is at stake for the opponent.

Whether an opponent can be motivated to behave differently by using carrots instead of sticks has informed debates about using incentives to persuade Iran to renounce its nuclear enrichment program. Could a grand political and economic bargain that gives Iran a stake in the international political and economic system convince it to alter its behavior on the nuclear issue? With the strengthening of the hard-line conservatives in Tehran under the presidency of Mahmoud Ahmadinejad and the stiffening resolve of Supreme Leader, Grand Ayatollah Sayyid Ali Khamenei, it is highly unlikely that idea would fly now. Iran has too many reputational, political, and strategic interests at stake in its nuclear program to be offset by any grand economic bargain. Moreover it may be that the legitimacy of the current regime rests squarely on opposing the designs of the great powers, such that nothing could induce them to become more compliant.

But it is possible that in the future, the use of carrots may be more effective in swaying Iran's behavior than in the past. A combination of pressure applied by the United States, and the shifting geopolitical landscape created by the Arab Spring, could convince Iran's leaders that they have more to lose than gain by continuing on its nuclear path. Perhaps, when faced with the tradeoff between the interests of economic prosperity and the prestige of a nuclear program, Iran would opt for economic prosperity. The economic sanctions imposed by the West are having a significant effect on the country's overall economy, and certainly were a factor in Iran's willingness to conduct negotiations in Istanbul,

Baghdad, and Moscow in 2012. The regional shifts that are occurring in the Middle East are also factors. The likely collapse of Syrian president Assad's government, which has served as Iran's conduit to Hezbollah and its only Arab ally, as well as the looming renaissance of Sunni Egypt bode poorly for Iran's regional position and even perhaps its internal legitimacy.[17] Iran's regional isolation, when coupled with increasingly punitive economic sanctions, could impel Iran to choose the interests of regime legitimacy and economic prosperity over national prestige. Under these conditions it might be possible to test whether carrots in addition to sticks can force tradeoffs between competing interests such that Iran's behavior will change.

Altering the Opponent's Perception of Threat of Opportunity

Another mechanism for influencing the behavior of an opponent is to alter its perception of threat or opportunity. Here the idea is to not to force tradeoffs between competing interests, but instead to alter the intensity with which the opponent perceives threat or opportunity to those interests. The assumption behind this kind of approach is that changes in the intensity of perceived opportunity or threat will have a causal effect on the opponent's behavior. The idea is to raise the opponent's perception of threat to dissuade it from taking undesirable actions, while lowering the threat, as well as creating a perception of opportunity, to encourage desirable actions.

The level of perceived threat or opportunity that triggers particular actions from an opponent is variable, depending on the type of leader at the helm. While a risk-averse leader may be influenced by verbal threats alone, a risk-prone opponent may be swayed only if that verbal threat is accompanied by a show of force. The risk-prone individual is more likely to interpret the verbal threat as a bluff or even be willing to tolerate the risk of confrontation. So in addition to calculating how a particular strategy will increase or decrease the perception of threat or opportunity, the strategist will need to assess the risk tolerance of the leadership. The degree of threat that would influence the behavior of a risk-prone leader like Saddam Hussein would need to be much higher than for a risk-averse leader like King Abdullah II of Jordan.

Libya's position on weapons of mass destruction in the wake of 9/11 is a good example. In the aftermath of the U.S. invasion of Afghanistan in 2001 and Iraq in 2003, Libya did an about-face. It dismantled its programs involving weapons of mass destruction and accepted responsibility for the 1988 bombing of Pan Am Flight 103 over Lockerbie, Scotland. This led to a normalization of relations between the United States and Libya in 2006.

What accounted for Qaddafi's abrupt volte-face? Was there a change in the way the Qaddafi government prioritized its interests? The demise of the Soviet Union led to an intensely perceived threat to Libya's security and economic interests over time. With the loss of its Soviet benefactor, Libya eventually became more isolated than ever before and had few allies it could rely on to help protect its security interests. Moreover, one of the costs of Libya's rogue behavior was that it was missing out on profitable foreign direct investments by Western international oil companies, something that impinged on its economic interests. What triggered the change, then, was not a shift in Libya's interests, rather a change in the perceived threat to those interests. The fact that the threshold for U.S. military action had gone down substantially since the events of 9/11 couldn't have been lost on the Qaddafi regime. Whether part of a U.S. strategy or just the result of a transformed post-9/11 environment, Qaddafi realized that he could no longer protect his security interests, advance his economic interests and maintain his current role as a regional pariah. The heightened threat in Libya's environment forced him to make a choice, which led to the dramatic change in the country's behavior.[18]

Breaking the Opponent's Morale or Will

While much of strategy deals with the more objective matters of interests and threats to those interests, the strategist trying to alter the motivation of an opponent should not forget the powerful role psychology and subjectivity play in the art of strategy. The strategist would be remiss in separating the objective interests of the opponent from the more subjective psychological lens through which its leaders perceive those interests.

The goal of strategies that target the psychological dynamics is to change, or in some cases break, the opponent's will to resist. Strategies can be aimed at the will of a political or business leader, or of the populace of a country. Famed French military strategist Gen. André Beaufre said it eloquently when he claimed, "the decision is obtained by creating and then exploiting a situation resulting in sufficient moral disintegration of the enemy to cause him to accept the conditions it is desired to impose on him."[19] For Beaufre the use of force can be effective in altering the psychological dynamics and breaking the will of an opponent.

How should the strategist be thinking about ways to use psychological mechanisms to alter the will of the opponent? There are a few different ways this can be done. We will address the use of strategic surprise and deception, as well as the deployment of overwhelming power in the pages that follow.

Strategies using the art of surprise and deception have been used in politics, international relations, business, and war for centuries. They are designed to catch the opponent unprepared, throw it off its game, immobilize it, and limit its ability to respond.[20] While deception and surprise are conceptually very different, they are interrelated in practice. Deceiving the opponent can be a necessary precursor to surprise—surprise can be thought of as the desired effect on the opponent, while deception is the method for achieving this effect.

There are several ways that the strategist can use deception to create surprise. The first is to maintain absolute secrecy about one's true intentions and plans. The combined Arab armies, led by Egypt and Syria, used surprise when they attacked Israel in October 1973 on Yom Kippur, the Jewish holiest day of the year. The Israeli Defense Forces were completely caught off guard and only gained the advantage after supply lines from the United States were established. The second is to telegraph false plans in an attempt to mislead the opponent as to one's actual intentions. While the enemy is not necessarily surprised, they are caught off guard by the specific path taken.[21] This was the approach the United States used in its planning for the invasion of Europe during World War II. The allied command deceived the Nazi government into believing that the U.S. invasion of France would take place near Calais, while in fact the venue was the coast of Normandy. They even put Gen. George Patton in Dover, England, right across from Calais, as a decoy to deceive the Nazis into believing that an invasion was about to take place there. While this didn't break the will of the enemy, it certainly gave the United States the strategic benefit of surprise and was a factor in the success of the invasion.

Another way to try to break the will of the opponent is to use overwhelming force. The use of overwhelming force can sometimes backfire and lead to increased resolve on the part of the opponent, but if it is sufficiently powerful it can have the desired effect by demonstrating the futility of resisting. For military or business leaders who have a significant advantage over the opponent in terms of power and resources, the use of overwhelming force can be one way to break the psychological will of the opponent. The initial U.S. foray into Baghdad during the 2003 invasion of Iraq used shock and awe tactics to break the will of the Iraqi government, and signal to the Iraqi people that the days of the regime of Saddam Hussein were numbered. While there was little strategic forethought given to how events would play out in the weeks and months following the invasion, the overwhelming use of force had the desired psychological effect of immobilizing the Iraqi military, the regime, and even the populace.

Disrupting the Strategy of the Opponent

Up to this point we have looked at strategic approaches for influencing the behavior of the opponent by either constraining its options, or affecting its motivation to choose certain options. But the strategist also needs to be prepared to counter the opponent's strategy, not just constrain its options to pursue that strategy.[22]

There are several ways to think about disrupting the opponent's strategy. The first is to counteract or block the opponent's ability to execute its strategy. In cases where interdicting the opponent's strategy is impossible, however, a second way is to interrupt the effectiveness of that strategy. The idea here is not to preclude the strategy, but rather to prevent it from being successful. A third way is to shift the opponent's strategy, pushing it in a less harmful direction. Let's briefly look at these different ways to disrupt the opponent's strategy.

Blocking the Opponent's Strategy

A battlefield example can illustrate the idea of providing a counterforce to blunt the enemy's strategy. An enemy military simultaneously launches land attacks on another country's three major cities and air attacks on its only port facility. The country trying to repel the attack instructs its army to meet the enemy troops that are en route to the three cities with a counterforce and instructs its air force to use its air defense systems to try to shoot down as many planes as possible. The country's strategy is to counteract the enemy's land and air attacks by interrupting the execution of the attacks.

Businesses, too, will try to interrupt the execution of their competitors' strategies. In the days of rapid retail expansion in the United States, chains like Home Depot or Wal-Mart would try to slow down their competitor's ability to enter new markets by buying prime real estate or signing leases for locations they might not plan to open up stores on for a number of years. They took this preemptive action to make their competitors' expansion strategies difficult, and force them to take less desirable locations when they did enter. While this seldom prevented the competitor retail chain from actually entering the new market, it did give the chain that arrived first a decisive advantage. It was a way to slow down, if not block, the execution of the competitor's strategy.

Minimizing the Effect of the Opponent's Strategy

In cases where stopping or even slowing down the opponent's strategy is not viable, another pathway is to think about reducing the effect of that strategy by cutting the link between the opponent's action and the outcome it desires. While the details of how to do this will be specific to individual situations there are some general principles. One is to design your strategy so that you are competing on your own terms, and not the opponent's. Much of business strategy is designed this way, where companies differentiate themselves to reduce the effectiveness of the opponent's strategy. Since companies can seldom stop their competitors from executing their strategies, they try to make their products and services sufficiently distinct, to prevent the competitor from taking their customers.

Another method is to alter the rules of the game to shift the battle toward your strengths and your opponent's weaknesses. If successful, the opponent can execute its strategy, but its effectiveness will be blunted. Take the Vietnam War for example—the North Vietnamese were masters at turning what U.S. military commanders considered strategic victories into mere tactical advantages. While they couldn't really counteract U.S. military actions, they were quite effective in blunting the effectiveness of the U.S. battlefield victories.

The 1968 Tet Offensive demonstrated that while it may have been impossible to blunt the force of U.S. military actions, there was still an opportunity for North Vietnamese victory by preventing these actions from achieving their desired effect. The North Vietnamese seemed to understand that the war was being fought on two fronts—one on the battlefields of Vietnam and the other on the political battleground in the United States and on American television. They realized that while they couldn't beat the United States militarily, they could probably still win by prolonging the conflict, thereby reducing the American people's will to continue fighting. The North Vietnamese were successfully able to prevent U.S. battlefield victories from translating into real strategic gains for the United States. Once public opinion turned against the war, any battlefield strategic advantages that had been achieved were neutralized in the political sphere.[23]

A few years after the Vietnam War ended an American colonel went to Hanoi to meet with his erstwhile enemy. A conversation ensued with the American colonel saying, "you know you never defeated us on the battlefield," to his Vietnamese counterpart. After hesitating for a moment, the Vietnamese colonel responded, "that may be so, but it is also irrelevant."[24] He meant that while the U.S. Army was successful on the battlefield, it was never able to turn this into strategic advantage, because the North Vietnamese were effective in blunting the effectiveness of the U.S. military strategy by focusing on, and understanding, the domestic political realm within which the strategy took place. They didn't win by matching force with force, but rather by changing the rules of engagement and winning on their own terms.

Shifting the Opponent's Strategy

A final way to disrupt an opponent's strategy is to shift it toward a less harmful direction. This is something that can be successful for both strong and weak players. While it may not be possible for a weaker player to interrupt the strategy of a stronger opponent, it may be possible to shift the direction of its opponent's strategy.

Confronting a more powerful actor is fraught with risk, but there are some ways to compensate for these power disparities. One is to provoke the opponent into making a move that will be self-defeating, shifting it off of a strategy that plays to its strengths and on to one that plays to its weaknesses. This could involve luring the opponent into a trap or getting it into a position such that its own strength gets used against it, effectively falling on its own sword. This move, known in martial arts as the jujitsu, entails using the overwhelmingly disproportionate power of the enemy against itself. Liddell Hart is more eloquent when he says, "so that as in ju-jitsu, his own effort is turned into the lever of his overthrow."[25]

Businesses also use these methods, drawing unwitting competitors into treacherous new markets in order to undermine them. Think of a company that enjoys high margins and is clearly the dominant force in its industry. A smaller competitor with inferior financial and market power knows that a frontal attack on the market of its larger rival would more than likely result in financial ruin, as the larger competitor would undoubtedly use its pricing power to undercut them. Instead the smaller company goes after a market niche that is either not served or underserved by the larger and more powerful rival.

But once the smaller company starts to build a viable business in the market's margins, the larger company takes notice. For the first time the large company focuses on this new market, launching an attack on the small company's customers. This move dilutes the larger company's focus, creating a wedge that can be exploited by the smaller company. After establishing a beachhead position on the margins of the market, the smaller company can compete in the core markets, challenging and weakening the larger company. So the small company used the power of the large company against itself, luring it away from its strategic sweet spot and having it weaken under its own weight.

CONCLUSION

This chapter doesn't claim to cover all possible strategic moves in the dimension of the opponent. But it hopefully is useful in sensitizing the strategist to thinking about the different ways to prevail over an opponent. We covered the three different ways to influence the behavior of or defeat an opponent. The first is to compromise the capability of the opponent. The second is to persuade the opponent to choose a particular option. And the third is to disrupt the strategy of the opponent. While these have been presented as distinct types of strategic concepts, they are not mutually exclusive. It is possible that a single strategy will embody all three strategic concepts, since a single strategy can work to disable the capability of the opponent, motivate it to act in a certain way, and counter its strategy.

One important caveat needs to be mentioned before leaving the realm of strategies aimed directly at the opponent—the opponent gets a vote as to how things unfold. The main difference between strategies in the system and opponent dimensions is that while the former only engages the opponent indirectly, the latter directly confronts it. This means that regardless of the robustness of your strategy, the opponent is going to respond in some way, which will require further strategic adjustment, as your moves will prompt countermoves. So your strategy will require agility and nimbleness to parry with the opponent as you try to influence its behavior and it tries to undermine you.[26]

5 STRATEGY IN THE DIMENSION OF GROUPS

Why are groups so important to the strategies of governments and businesses? The importance of groups to strategy is not new. Clausewitz in the nineteenth century expounded on the importance of the passion of the people as one element of his trinity of war. He argued that while war in the eighteenth century had excluded the people and been the exclusive purview of government, war in the nineteenth century needed to reflect more of a balance between the government, the army, and the people.[1] He in effect claimed that the people as a whole, and groups of organized citizens, needed to be factored into strategy.

While Clausewitz's writings teach us that that the reasons for making groups a primary dimension of strategy hark back to ancient times, the dynamics of the modern world tell us that groups should be elevated even higher in their importance to strategy. The emergence of mass politics and the phenomenon of democratization in the former Soviet Republics and Eastern Europe has been the impetus to increasing the importance of groups in political and national security strategies. Even authoritarian governments rely on either passive acquiescence or active support from their mass publics. One of the lessons of the Arab Spring, which began in 2011, is that once popular support is withdrawn, regimes can become unstable very quickly. Moreover, globalization and the prominence and ubiquity of the social media have led to an empowerment of mass publics, which can be either mobilized for or against leaders. These phenomena make groups even more strategically important. As either an asset or a liability for a leader of a country, groups can be effective instruments of strategy.

A similar dynamic has arisen in global business environments. Consumer groups, with the help of NGOs, can mobilize public opinion for or against global companies, with real implications for their brand, reputation, and balance sheets. Thanks to social media, consumers and concerned citizens can organize and shape the destiny of powerful companies. Moreover, the emergence of global mass-markets makes understanding the behavior of groups even more important. A corporate leader interested in acquiring or sustaining a competitive advantage must understand the differences and similarities of groups of consumer segments across broad swaths of geography and culture.

For our purposes, a group is defined as a collection of individuals that can affect the leverage dynamic between an organization or country against its opponents. In the foreign policy milieu these groups can be civil society groups, political parties, or opposition groups within an opponent's domestic political system. They could also be groups within one's own political system whose support is needed by leaders in order to pursue a particular foreign policy.[2] On the business front they may be groups of employees, customers, consumer groups, or other stakeholders that can affect the brand or the legitimacy of a company or its competitor.

So what does strategy at the level of the group look like? Like strategy in the dimension of the system, group strategies are indirect in that they don't aim directly at the opponent, but rather at its environment. The idea is to take aim at the groups that add to or subtract from an opponent's leverage.[3] On the foreign policy side, these generally fall within the purview of public diplomacy and strategic communications strategies, which aim to weaken the opponent by mobilizing its own constituent groups against it.[4] On the business side, these types of strategies involve deploying highly sophisticated and targeted campaigns aimed at building support among consumer or citizen groups for a company's initiatives, for staving off challenges from NGOs, or for building support for a particular corporate social responsibility initiative.[5] They can also be used to target specific groups of market segments on behalf of a new product launch.

There are several caveats that need to be stated about these types of strategies. The first is that the time frame for these strategies tends to be medium to long term, meaning they are not quick fixes. Messages aimed at groups only resonate if the sender has a semblance of legitimacy, which can take time to establish. Moreover, to be effective, communication strategies aimed at internal or external audiences need to be carefully planned, meticulously executed, and sustained over long periods of time. Cultivating groups, and developing lines of communication that resonate, requires a great deal of patience and the luxury of time.

The second caveat is that these types of strategies are seldom effective on a stand-alone basis. To be effective, strategic moves in the dimension of groups need to be a part of a broader set of system and opponent level strategies. Group strategies often fail because too much burden has been placed on them. Public diplomacy strategies that aren't nested in a broader grand strategy are likely to be ineffective because they alone can't move the leverage needle far enough.[6] They can reinforce but not replace strategies aimed directly at an opponent or at its external systems environment.

The third caveat is that strategies in the dimension of groups, which rely heavily on communication, need to be backed up with decisive action to be effective. On the government side, messages aimed at groups can signal a policy but cannot be a substitute for policy; they need to be reinforced with action. On the business side, marketing and corporate social responsibility strategies need to be integrated into and backed up with broader strategic initiatives. If they are deemed to be superficial or disingenuous by audiences, they will be rendered ineffective and can even make matters worse for the company.

GROUP STRATEGIES

The first step to using strategy in the dimension of groups is to identify which groups might be candidates for your strategy. There are generally two criteria for this. The first is that the group must be accessible to you and have reasons to be receptive to your influence. The second is that the group must have the potential to affect your leverage against the opponent, which involves identifying the individual groups, or network of groups, that currently support the opponent. While these groups may represent strength for the opponent, they also present a vulnerability that potentially could be exploited. It also involves identifying groups that may not actually support the opponent, but whose passivity the opponent counts on for stability. These are groups whose mobilization against the opponent could potentially threaten its stability and compromise its leverage. Groups that are actively opposing the opponent should also be identified and flagged. The strategist will need to decide whether these opposition groups can be strengthened or supported to become an even more formidable force against the opponent.

Groups can fall into two different broad categories—they can either be formal groups with some kind of hierarchical structure, or informal groups composed of individuals who share a common belief, orientation, or characteristic, but have little in the way of organizational structure.

Strategies for Formal Groups

Let's start with an analysis of formal groups, which are characterized by some form of organizational structure and leadership. Formal groups also have clear boundaries in terms of who is and is not a member and typically have a set of expressed institutional interests and purposes. Political parties, civil societies, NGOs, and advocacy groups are all examples of formal groups.

Before creating a strategy, there are several questions that need to be answered about formal groups. The first is what are the interests of the group that will motivate it to work with you? The second is what capabilities does it have to affect your opponent? The third is does the group have pragmatic factions that would likely respond positively to your efforts to weaken the opponent? And finally, who specifically within the group will be the target of your strategy?

Let's look at a foreign policy case to demonstrate how this kind of analysis can be done. The Key Leader Engagement initiative, otherwise known as the Sunni Awakening, led by Gen. David Petraeus in Iraq in 2006–2007 is an example of how formal groups can be chosen based on a mutuality of interests and their capability to degrade an opponent.

The primary opponent to the United States in this case was al-Qaeda. In order to exploit the situation of chaos in Iraq, al-Qaeda had aligned itself with Sunni insurgent groups and tribes that had become disillusioned with, and disenfranchised from, the Shi'i led government that took power following the overthrow of Saddam Hussein. These Sunni groups were key to al-Qaeda's leverage in Iraq because their alliance with the terrorist group amplified its effect. Because of this,

Petraeus and others viewed these groups as potential targets of a strategy to defeat al-Qaeda in Iraq. The logic was that if the Sunni groups could be somehow persuaded to withdraw support from al-Qaeda, the terrorist group's stature and power would be significantly weakened in Iraq.

As with all group strategies, the first question needs to be, what interests would motivate the Sunni groups to share common cause with the U.S. government? Given their affiliation with al-Qaeda, why would Sunni groups switch loyalties and now agree to work with the U.S. military? Let's look at their interests. Sunni leaders were concerned about protecting several interests, including the maintenance of their legitimacy and support among the civilian Sunni population.[7] There was some risk that a continued relationship with al-Qaeda could potentially erode that support, given the terrorist group's use of wanton violence in Iraq. Because of this, the Sunni insurgency groups that had initially supported al-Qaeda had started to become disillusioned.

An even more critical interest for the Sunnis, however, was gaining more influence in what had become a Shi'i dominated central government. Their association with al-Qaeda had been more of a means to exert power over the Iraqi government, than an end itself. While the Sunni insurgents' interests involved restoring lost political influence in the government, al-Qaeda's goal was to create instability and prevent any government from governing. Because of these divergent interests, the sheiks of the various Sunni groups were predisposed to pull back from a relationship with al-Qaeda and work with the U.S. military.[8]

Now let's move from the analysis of the interests and capabilities of the group to the strategy stage. To do this you need to answer several questions. What is the goal for the strategy? In other words, what outcome are you trying to achieve with the opponent. Is the goal to defeat the opponent, or merely weaken it and decrease its bargaining leverage?

Next you need to determine the aim of the strategy, which is different than the goal. Think of the aim as the behavior your strategy is designed to elicit from the group, while the goal is the impact that behavior should have on the opponent. Is the aim to have the group withdraw support from, or actively oppose, the opponent? Or is to have the group cajole other groups in an attempt to weaken the opponent?

The third question is what specific methods will be used to influence the behavior of the group. Will the methods be co-optation using incentives or will coercion be used? And what are the specifics of the methods? Will the strategy involve merely working with the leadership of the group, or also its rank and file?

The final question is what assumptions are being made as to why your strategy will ultimately succeed. There are two parts to this. The first is why will your strategy achieve the desired effect on the group's behavior? The second is assuming the strategy has the desired effect on the behavior of the group, how will this actually have the intended effect on the opponent? What assumptions are being made about the vulnerability or strength of the opponent, and the ability of the group to exploit these?

So let's use these questions about goals, aims, methods, and assumptions to further examine General Petraeus's military strategy in Iraq from 2006–2008 of co-opting the Sunni groups that had joined al-Qaeda.[9]

What were the goals of the strategy of targeting Sunni groups? The first was to weaken and ultimately defeat al-Qaeda in Iraq, while the second was to stabilize the fledgling Iraqi government. Assuming the Sunni leaders and their constituencies would respond favorably, achieving these goals seemed realistic. As previously mentioned, the Sunnis had provided the much needed local support to al-Qaeda and also had directly challenged the Shi'i led Iraqi government. Successful co-optation of the Sunni sheikhs would deprive al-Qaeda of the much-needed on-the-ground support and also would remove a source of pressure on the Iraqi government.

What were the aims of the strategy, meaning what behavior was the military trying to elicit from the Sunni groups? The first was to get the Sunni sheiks to collaborate with the Americans in their fight against al-Qaeda. As part of this, an ancillary, secondary aim was to get the various Sunni groups to form coalitions in order to create a more effective phalanx against al-Qaeda. The third aim was to get the Sunni groups to start the process of reconciliation with the Iraqi government. Petraeus wanted the Sunnis to first withhold support from and even fight al-Qaeda, and then eventually shift their loyalties to the Iraqi government.

What methods were used to co-opt the Sunni groups? The methods the U.S. military used fell into a few different categories. The first was the use of inducements (popularly referred to as carrots), the second was the use of force (popularly referred to as sticks), and the third was the reinforcement of mutual interests.

The United States used carrots in the form of direct cash payments to the leaders and junior officials of the Sunni groups. Dubbed "rent a sheikh," financial incentives were used to align the interests of the groups with the interests of the U.S. military. Long-term financial investments were also made in critical public work projects in Sunni controlled areas.[10] Opportunities for employment were another form of financial incentive. Non-financial carrots were also used to integrate Sunni groups into an anti al-Qaeda force. One of these was to allow the groups to protect their own communities.[11] Another was for the military to convince recalcitrant Shi'i groups, as well as Iraqi government coalition groups, to reconcile with the Sunni leadership and their constituents. The idea was that if the Sunni leaders no longer felt threatened, and believed they had something to gain within the Iraqi political context, they would have an incentive to cooperate with the United States.[12]

In addition to carrots, the U.S. military used sticks in the form of implicit and sometimes explicit threats to Sunni groups that chose to be uncooperative. To reinforce this, the Sunni groups that were thought to be irreconcilable were targeted for lethal force.[13] While explicit threats were seldom used against Sunni leaders who were thought to be reconcilable, the knowledge that the U.S. military was targeting irreconcilable groups certainly sharpened the implicit message.

In addition to using carrots and sticks the military also reinforced the interests of the Sunni groups that motivated them to work with the United States. Strategic communications and public diplomacy were used to show that there was a commonality of interests between the Sunni groups and the U.S. military. The military targeted several messages at the Sunni leaders and their constituents to reinforce these common interests and drive a wedge between these groups and al-Qaeda. While Sunni leader disillusionment with al-Qaeda had set in before the U.S. strategy commenced, these messages accelerated and reinforced the strain. The first type of message highlighted the atrocities perpetrated on Sunni leaders by al-Qaeda. One of the most notorious and flagrant was al-Qaeda's assassination of Sheik Nasr, head of the Sunni Albu Fahd tribe, after he and other Sunni tribal leaders met with the U.S. ambassador to Iraq, Zalmay Khalilzad.[14] The second message communicated that an al-Qaeda controlled enclave in Anbar province intended to wrest political control away from Sunni tribal leaders. This rankled the Sunni leaders as much as or more than the atrocities against innocents. All of these messages were aimed at reinforcing the mutual interests that were evolving between the Sunni groups and the U.S. military.

Success of any group strategy needs to be measured by whether it has met its aims with the targeted group and its goals against the opponent. Was the U.S. strategy successful in achieving its aims relative to the Sunni groups? As far as effectively mobilizing the Sunni groups, the strategy was quite successful. The combination of carrots, sticks, and mutual interests clearly had the desired impact on the behavior of the Sunni groups. They organized themselves into national coalitions, such as the Reformation and Jihad Front, the Jihad and Change Front, and the Supreme Council of Jihad and Liberation. They also formed the first umbrella Sunni organization, the Political Council for the Iraqi Resistance.[15] The Sunni groups did this mostly to position themselves to more effectively combat al-Qaeda and be able to defend their own communities from Shi'i militias. So, it appears that the assumptions made by the U.S. military about mobilizing the Sunni groups seemed to hold, and that the strategy's aims were met. Also, given al-Qaeda's setbacks in Iraq, particularly in Anbar province, and its inability to sabotage the Iraqi government, it seems that the goal of undermining al-Qaeda was met.

However, the assumption that co-opting the Sunni tribal leaders and isolating al-Qaeda would achieve the goal of strengthening the Iraqi government was more problematic. This is because the stability of the Iraqi government depended on more than removing the threat of al-Qaeda and the Sunni insurgency. There were also Shi'i militant groups and infighting within the government that contributed to the government's instability. But given the potency of al-Qaeda and the number of Sunni groups that had been disenfranchised from the political system, it seems clear that weakening al-Qaeda, and co-opting the Sunnis at least made some dent in stabilizing the Iraqi government, at least in the short to medium term.

Now let's shift gears and move to how businesses can use formal groups to their advantage. It is not uncommon for business leaders to scan their environments looking for groups that can buttress the position of their companies. A corporate executive, for example, might look for non-profit organizations that can lend credibility to a company's claims that it behaves in a socially responsible way. It could also be done to undercut efforts by the competition to challenge the company's brand and reputation.

Starbucks Coffee Company's effort to make support for the environment and the welfare of small coffee producers part of its brand promise is an example of this type of strategy. Part of this initiative involved aligning with the non-profit organization Conservation International. Aside from Starbucks's wanting to become a socially responsible company, another motivation for this strategy was risk mitigation. Because the company had publicly stated that its values involved social and environmental responsibility, it could be vulnerable to charges from competitors and NGOs that its practices didn't live up to its publicity. Given the power and value of the Starbucks brand, this scrutiny had the potential to hurt the company's reputation and even its competitive advantage in the industry. Starbucks concluded that an alliance with Conservation International would lend credence to its claims, help it sustain its brand advantage, and better enable it to withstand assaults by competitors and activist groups.[16]

Like in the case of Iraq, before forming an alliance with Conservation International, Starbucks would have had to analyze the NGO's interests and motivation. What ultimately made Conservation International a viable partner was its aspiration to set up industry guidelines to promote shade grown coffee and protect the environment. Conservation International's interests had pushed it to launch a Center for Environmental Leadership in Business (CELB), whose mission was to engage with businesses on behalf of solving global environmental problems.[17] It had chosen coffee production as a key area for focus, and Starbucks represented approximately 1 percent of global coffee sales, making the chain attractive as a partner to the NGO, and vice versa.[18]

The goal of Starbucks's strategy with Conservation International was ultimately to protect its brand from visible attacks by activist organizations. Its aim with respect to Conservation International was to get positive media coverage through, and perhaps even an implied endorsement from, the non-profit organization. It also hoped to learn something from the pilot project it established with Conservation International that could be later be expanded to a larger scale.

In terms of the methods Starbucks used, the initiative relied on mutual interests, not on any carrots or sticks. Starbucks had its brand

and corporate reputation at stake, and Conservation International's mission was to limit the environmental damage done to rain forests by the coffee industry. Starbucks needed the credibility offered by tacit endorsements from the non-profit organization, and Conservation International needed the scale of Starbucks to get sufficient traction for its conservation program. Once the partnership built on mutual interests was formed, Starbucks worked with Conservation International to develop environmental standards that could be relayed to coffee farmers in Mexico. In addition, Starbucks worked closely with the non-profit organization to develop new coffee-purchasing guidelines.[19]

What were the assumptions behind Starbucks' strategy of working with Conservation International as a risk mitigation strategy? It assumed that the project to train coffee farmers, the new coffee sourcing procedures, and the introduction of more environmentally friendly purchasing guidelines, would be visible enough to redound positively to Starbucks' reputation. In other words, the assumption was that these efforts were significant enough to protect the company's brand in the eyes of the press and consumers, and that consumers would vote with their pocketbooks and continue to favor Starbucks Coffee. The strategy also assumed that the partnership with Conservation International would be robust enough to dilute the effects of more activist organizations, which might see Starbucks as a large target. If the association with Conservation International had made Starbucks a bigger, but no less vulnerable target for activist groups, then this assumption would have been wrong and the strategy would have been a failure.[20] While there were attacks by other NGOs on Starbucks's reluctance to institute Fair Trade sourcing practices, the relationship with Conservation International nonetheless helped the company mitigate risk to its brand and helped it to establish best practices.

In sum, identifying and analyzing formal groups requires one to answer several questions—which groups have the potential to change the leverage dynamics of the opponent, which groups may be motivated to act in the desired way, and what interests or grievances can be exploited in a possible strategy. Launching a strategy for formal groups requires the strategist to identify the goal of the strategy, the aim for the group, the methods used for targeting the group and the assumptions about how the strategy will work. The Sunni Awakening and Starbucks cases illustrate how this can be done.

Strategies for Informal Groups

While formal groups present an important focus of strategy, they don't represent the entire universe of groups. The strategist should also look for informal groups that could have strategic value. But there is a wide spectrum within this category. On one end are groups of loosely affiliated individuals galvanized around a common cause, like the fledgling reformist movements that challenged the Egyptian government during the Arab Spring. At the other end of the spectrum are informal groups composed of individuals who are completely unaware of their inclusion in the group and who remain unaffiliated with each other. We only consider these collections of individuals as groups because of some shared characteristic or sentiment that might make the individual members receptive to some form of collective action or mobilization.

One example of this latter type of group would be independent voters in a political campaign, who may be strategically significant for a particular candidate because of a common set of behavioral, socio-economic, and ideological characteristics, but may not be affiliated with one another. They may be seen as a group by campaign officials, because of a common attribute like income, a need such as assistance with finding employment opportunities, or a particular political behavior. On the foreign policy side, an example of this type of informal group might be the youth in Iran, bound by the common characteristics of age, education, and reform-mindedness. While they may not be affiliated with any particular party, they might become strategically significant for the United States if they have the capability and motivation to put pressure on the Iranian regime. An example on the business side is how companies group consumers into market segments. That is, based on need, attributes, or behavior, subsets of a given population become targets for products or marketing campaigns. An illustration might be the customer segment group targeted by luxury carmakers like BMW, Mercedes, and Lexus. Their customers certainly share the attributes of being in the upper income echelons and valuing luxury and status. While the members of this market segment group are not aware of each other, they still form a distinct target segment group for luxury carmakers.[21]

It has been said that strategy involves the skills of the scientist as well as the finesse of the artist.[22] While this is apropos to all types of strategy, it rings particularly true with strategies involving informal groups. Strategy in this domain involves targeting loosely organized groups that have little or no leadership. It also entails targeting like-minded individuals who, despite sharing a common characteristic or attitude, are unaffiliated with one another and unaware that they are considered a member of a group. With loosely organized groups the challenge is how they can be reached and mobilized, while for groups of unaffiliated individuals bound only by some common characteristic, the challenge is how to imagine them and tap into their collective power.

Imagining the potential of informal groups to create competitive advantage is what consummate marketers of products and services do for a living. They identify groups, or segments, of consumers and then develop products, services, and marketing campaigns around their particular characteristics, behaviors, or needs. Political campaign strategists similarly use the power of informal groups to create competitive advantage over their candidate's political rivals. Based on sophisticated models and algorithms that take into account attitudinal, demographic, and socio-economic attributes, individuals are assigned to different voter segments. Campaign strategists then develop strategies for reaching these different voter segments. While it may remain opaque to individual voters how they are categorized, they are nonetheless targeted with tailored messages designed to get them to vote for their candidate.

Much of what is done in foreign policy with public diplomacy and strategic communications is also targeted at informal groups.[23] Although governments use public diplomacy on behalf of a broad range of political objectives, one particular purpose is to put pressure on and reduce the leverage of foreign governments and non-state actors. Strategies using these methods involve crafting messages and actions for either broad, or in some cases narrow, audiences.[24]

Like with strategies for formal groups, before embarking on a strategy aimed at informal groups, several questions need to be answered. How will the group be defined, what are the goals and aims of the strategy, what methods will be used, and what are the underlying assumptions of the strategy?

The first step in defining the group is to decide how wide to cast the net in terms of the scope of the group to be targeted. Unlike formal groups, which have clear boundaries, the contours of informal groups are more subjective. Because strategy at this level primarily involves communication tools, it is important that the strategist be clear about who the core part of the audience is.

Companies have to answer the question about how they define their target market groups. The classic example of this is a global company that targets its marketing efforts at consumers with a particular income or socioeconomic profile. The company tailors its messages, products, and energies to the needs or behaviors of that particular segment. The justification for a company concentrating its effort on specific groups of customers is that it will lead to better results than a more generalized, diffused campaign.

Think about the market segments targeted by Apple with the iPhone. When the product first launched in 2007 the phone's $400 retail price indicated that the company was interested in market segments that included individuals who earned medium and high incomes, early adopters of new technology, and die-hard Apple fans. Apple believed that by targeting this smaller market segment, it could generate the greatest sales and build a foundation upon which it could later expand. While the company later expanded its target market to include groups of lower income consumers, by offering older iPhone models for $100, it felt that it was important to initially focus on a narrower market segment of more affluent users.

On the government side, public diplomacy and strategic communications strategists need to define their target groups using similar methods. While some of the policies and messages are aimed at broad audiences, others are aimed at narrower demographic segments. In the case of the U.S. public diplomacy strategy aimed at attacking al-Qaeda, certain populations that are vulnerable to extremism have been specifically targeted. Policymakers have narrowed this further, targeting the youth, women, and minorities. The logic of the youth segment would be that although it might be the most impressionable and susceptible to extremism, through education and the media it could also be the most receptive to attitudinal changes. The women segment would be included because of the belief that they could be positive forces for change, leading societies towards greater stability and moderation. The minorities could be targeted because they tend to be the most disenfranchised elements of the society and therefore might be predisposed to mobilization by terrorist groups.[25]

Another question that needs to be answered is whether individuals of the informal group will be targeted directly, or should they be targeted indirectly through opinion makers? This decision should be made on the basis of an assessment of your capability to reach the individuals of the group, as well as your ability to influence their attitudes and beliefs. In cases where this is dubious, it might be more effective to instead target someone who holds sway over the opinions and attitudes of the group. U.S. policymakers may conclude they lack the capacity to counter the virulently anti-American messages spewed by al-Qaeda and militant clerics in the Middle East. So instead of directly focusing on the masses, they may consider focusing efforts on certain moderate Islamic leaders, journalists, and business leaders who could be inclined to peddle a less hostile narrative. While these moderate leaders certainly wouldn't sway the opinion of the most radicalized segments of society, targeting them might be more effective in influencing mainstream attitudes than a direct American communications campaign.[26]

Corporate marketers have to make similar determinations about whether to target informal groups directly or through opinion-makers. Pharmaceutical companies, for example, have to decide how much of their advertising budgets to expend on direct marketing to physicians and how much to allocate to consumers watching late-night television. The idea behind targeting consumers is that they will place pressure on and influence the behavior of the physicians. In this case, the consumers are the influencers or opinion-makers, and the physicians with the discretion to prescribe, the ultimate targets of the strategy. While targeting physician and consumer audiences are not mutually exclusive methods, a pharmaceutical company will need to decide where the emphasis of its strategy should be placed.

Another question that needs to be addressed before launching a strategy is what are the aims for the informal group? There are different types of aims for strategies targeting informal groups. One is activation, meaning that the aim of the strategy is to mobilize the group into action. This might involve mobilizing a previously inactive group or population into action against their government. Another is pacification, meaning getting a group or population that actively supported their government to withdraw that support. Consider a public diplomacy strategy aimed at Muslim populations where the goal is to defeat al-Qaeda. Would the aim of the strategy be to actively mobilize the masses against the jihadist group? Or would the aim be to merely pacify them into not actively opposing U.S. interests in the region? More than likely the aim would be one of pacification and making the populations more resistant to extremist ideology and action. For a consumer products company targeting a particular market segment, the aim of the strategy would be activation into certain buying behaviors.

The question of what methods will be used to elicit the desired response from the group also needs to be answered. Strategic methods for informal groups tend to fall into two different categories. The first is communication methods, which involves the dissemination of messages to target audiences, including the crafting of the specific content of the messages. The second is the policy actions designed to reinforce the messages that have been delivered to the target audience.

Much of the thinking on public diplomacy strategy posits that communication methods are necessary but insufficient in terms of achieving aims. In public diplomacy it is particularly important that the communication and action methods reinforce one another. In other words, messages need to be backed up with policy changes and clear and visible action.[27] If the message of a U.S. public diplomacy strategy aimed at Muslim women and youth is that the behavior of al-Qaeda is violent, the actions that might complement this would be things that would paint the United States in a more benign, positive light. These actions might include development programs, such as building women's centers, and establishing schools for the youth. While the messaging component of the strategy places al-Qaeda in a negative light, the action component is designed to put the United States in a positive light.

The last question is, what assumptions are you making as to how your strategy is designed to work? It is important to show how the strategic methods will achieve both the aims you have for the group as well as the goals for influencing the opponent. To illustrate this, let's continue looking at a U.S. strategy for dealing with the threat from al-Qaeda. Let's assume that the aim is to make certain Muslim mass public groups less receptive to the extremist views of al-Qaeda. In order for the strategy to work, there needs to be some receptivity to the messages on the part of the target audiences. Why would one ever assume that a public diplomacy strategy could work when anti-American sentiments have been so embedded in the political culture of this region? Up until now there has been little encouragement in this regard. U.S. military involvements in Iraq and Afghanistan and support for reactionary Arab governments have reinforced the well-entrenched political narratives that feed extremist views. The broad historical narrative of exploitation of Moslem groups by the United States painted by jihadist groups to justify their actions resonate with a wide mainstream audience, even though the violent methods they use are condoned by only a small percentage of the overall population. Under these conditions public diplomacy and strategic communications alone have little chance in swinging hearts and minds.

But oftentimes, acting strategically with informal groups means waiting for conditions in the environment to improve. While a public diplomacy strategy alone won't be effective in countering the well-embedded extremist narrative, there may be an opportunity lurking in the shadows of the Arab Spring that could translate into a net loss for al-Qaeda and other extremist groups. The fact that secular Arab protesters in Egypt and Tunisia were able to accomplish, using mostly peaceful means what extremist Islamic groups like al-Qaeda could not deliver using violent means, has the potential to dilute the effectiveness of the extremist narrative. While al-Qaeda may yet benefit from the chaos in Syria and other Arab countries, so far it has not been able to hijack the Arab Spring.

In light of these developments, it is possible that al-Qaeda could be weakened further by a combination of well-designed and executed U.S. public diplomacy strategic moves. There could be an opportunity for U.S. actions, reinforced by clearly articulated messages, to loosen the deeply held extremist views, something that previous policies have been unable to achieve. U.S. support for NATO's role in the overthrow of Qaddafi in Libya, and U.S. statements calling for President Assad of Syria to step down, provide an opportunity to change this narrative and contribute to a regional environment less fertile for al-Qaeda's ideology.

CONCLUSION

Strategy in the dimension of the group can be a powerful form of indirect strategy. It is a form of strategy that recognizes and leverages the power of individuals, formally or informally organized into groups. These strategies can work by either mobilizing, or in some case pacifying, groups that affect the power dynamics of opponents.

The one caveat is that these strategies generally need to be part of a broader, overarching strategy consisting of strategies in the dimensions of systems and opponents. While seldom effective unless reinforced by other strategies, group strategies can be an potent part of the business or foreign policy practitioner's strategic toolbox.

PART 3

THE POWER OF INTEGRATION

6 | AL-QAEDA'S STRATEGY IN 3D

This book has made the argument that the strategist should be looking for strategic opportunities and threats in the dimensions of the system, the opponent, and the group. It has also provided examples of how in foreign policy, national security, and business, strategy can play out in each of these dimensions. We have seen that while strategy in the dimensions of the system and the group engages the adversary only indirectly, strategy in the dimension of the opponent involves direct engagement and sometimes even confrontation. And while strategy in the dimensions of the group and the system generally involve longer time horizons, strategy at the level of the opponent can be short, medium, or long term.

THE POWER OF INTEGRATION

What hasn't been addressed yet is how strategy in these different dimensions can conspire to create the much-desired multiplier effect. While we have discussed how strategy works in each of these dimensions, we haven't delved into how the different dimensions of strategy interrelate and work together.

Strategy in 3D is similar to playing three different games simultaneously, each taking place in a different dimension of the strategic environment. While not every situation demands action in each dimension, the strategist should at least be scanning all three for threats or opportunities. Strategic success can depend on the compounding effect of successes in each of the dimensions, while failure can come, despite success in one dimension, because of losses in the other dimensions. The strategist intent on increasing the probability of success, and reducing the probability of failure, can ill afford to ignore any of these dimensions of the strategic environment.

Some strategies require success in all dimensions of the strategic environment. Other strategies can achieve success despite a setback in one or even two of the dimensions. The former are formulaic strategies, which work because of how the three different strategic elements interact with one another, fusing almost into a single strategy. Like a recipe, where one missing ingredient can ruin the culinary dish, failure in one dimension can mean overall strategic failure. The upshot of this is that formulaic strategies tend to be all-or-nothing propositions, with no such thing as partial success.

By contrast, partial success is possible despite a failure in one of the dimensions with independent strategies. While success may be greater with traction created in all three dimensions, it is not required. With independent strategies, the system, opponent, and group levels work independently toward a common goal.

How does this notion of formulaic versus independent strategies relate to the real worlds of foreign policy and business? While there is no universal rule, formulaic strategies tend to apply in strategic situations where success can't really be measured in degrees and where a tipping point is required in order to pressure an opponent to take a particular action.[1] Getting Iran to renounce its nuclear enrichment program may be just such a scenario. The concept behind a strategy for achieving this goal is to build sufficient pressure on the Iranian leadership so that they make a decision they would not otherwise make. The range of possible outcomes will be largely binary; the Iranian government will make a decision to continue on its present path, or will negotiate on its nuclear enrichment program. If this goal can be achieved, it will only occur because maximum pressure has been built on the Iranian government. This pressure means working indirectly and directly, creating traction at the system, opponent, and group levels. Unless Russia and China agree to apply pressure (system dimension), the United States continues targeted economic sanctions (opponent dimension), and internal political constituencies put pressure on the regime (group dimension), a change in Iran's position is unlikely. With a formulaic strategy like this, success will be elusive unless all cylinders of the strategy are firing. There is no such thing as partial success.

When strategies for a particular goal are independent of one another success can generally be measured in degrees. As long as one of the strategic dimensions delivers traction, some progress toward the goal can be achieved. Take, for example, the goal of reducing the number of attacks by the Taliban against civilian populations in Afghanistan by 75 percent. Assume there are system, opponent, and group strategies deployed to reach this goal. The system strategy would involve working with regional powers like Pakistan, which can influence the flow of men, weaponry, and material across the Afghan-Pakistan border. This strategy alone could lead to some decline in the number of attacks, though certainly not 75 percent. Strategy in the dimension of the opponent would involve the United States and NATO trying to directly cripple the Taliban's capability by attacking its strongholds. Largely independent of any pressure on Pakistan, this strategic path also has the potential to decrease the number of attacks. Strategy in the dimension of groups would involve working with the Afghan government and civilian groups to protect villages from attack, which could also contribute to lower the number of attacks. These are three different strategies, but each contributes to a reduced number of civilian attacks. While failure at one level will reduce the degree of success, it won't necessarily translate into absolute failure.

Should strategy in each of the dimensions be executed simultaneously, or be sequenced? And if they are sequenced, does the order matter? Like with most questions about strategy, the answer depends on the situation. It may be irrelevant if the strategist doesn't have the time to sequence strategies. Timelines may be so compressed that strategy in each of the dimensions get conflated and overlap with one another. If there are opportunities for sequencing different strategies, the optimal order will depend on the strategic situation and how the opponent derives leverage. If your strategy is aimed at an intrinsically weak opponent that derives most of its leverage from its external environment, then it is unlikely that strategies aimed directly at it will work until the links to its external sources of leverage have been interdicted. In this kind of situation, system strategies ideally take place first in the sequence. Moreover, since system strategies tend to have a longer time horizon, they would ideally be launched far in advance of strategies aimed directly at the opponent. But with a powerful opponent that derives most of its leverage from its own intrinsic capability, it is unlikely that real strategic progress will be made until it is engaged directly. So in this case, the argument of starting with a system strategy is less compelling. Answers to the question of timing are dependent on the particular circumstances and the timelines involved.

AL-QAEDA'S STRATEGY IN 3D

To illustrate further the power of integration, we will examine a case involving strategy in all three of the dimensions. This will be al-Qaeda's strategy against the United States for the period leading up to the attacks on September 11, 2001, as well as in the aftermath of those events. This case has been chosen for several reasons. The first is that it provides a useful complement to the examples used in earlier chapters about the U.S. strategy for al-Qaeda. There is benefit in now turning the tables and looking at al-Qaeda's view of the strategic situation and at its strategic plans. Moreover, because al-Qaeda was the first truly global terrorist organization, analyzing its strategy in a systematic way has the added benefit of giving us insight into how international crime or terror organizations might think in the future.[2] This case also demonstrates that the framework can be useful not just in the preparation of one's own strategy but also in creating insights into the opponent's strategy.

Despite the fact that there has been an abundance of research and analysis about al-Qaeda's strategy, there is still a lot we don't know. We don't know the motivation behind the posting of what appears to be al-Qaeda's playbook on the Internet in 2004.[3] Was this an officially sanctioned act by the senior leadership team of al-Qaeda or the work of a lone wolf? Or, was it a deliberate attempt to throw up a smokescreen to confuse U.S. and other Western national security planners? Most of the documents lacked timelines and operational detail, so we don't know how much of what is stated is aspirational and how much actually reflects the terrorist organization's operational readiness.

Since our purpose is to illustrate the strategy framework outlined in the previous chapters, these gaps in our understanding about the motivation behind, and provenance of, these documents are not particularly troublesome or debilitating to our effort to model how al-Qaeda's strategy functioned.

Al-Qaeda's Strategic Goals

What al-Qaeda's goals were is still up for interpretation, because it is difficult to distinguish between the terrorist group's aspirations and its actual strategic goals. We know that al-Qaeda aspired to establish a new Islamic Caliphate that spans the entire Islamic world.[4] But was this tantamount to a grand strategy goal for al-Qaeda, or merely a lofty aspirational objective that was cast far into the future? It is unclear to what extent al-Qaeda's operational plans and thinking went toward this goal. We know that one of the terrorist organization's goals involved the destabilization and ultimate collapse of conservative Arab states in the region. We also believe that al-Qaeda was motivated by a belief that inflicting considerable damage onto the United States hastens the day when these Arab regimes will collapse. The logic being that the support from the United States is what props up these conservative states, and that a United States on the defensive will be unable to adequately protect these regimes. While al-Qaeda's long-term goal for the United States may have been defeat, its medium-range objectives were to get the superpower to jettison its alliances with reactionary Arab regimes in the region and pull up its roots in the Middle East.[5] In other words, while al-Qaeda saw the United States as its main far enemy, it also had its sights on its near enemies, which were the conservative Arab regimes.[6] Part of the strategy for defeating the near enemy was to inflict damage, destruction, and even defeat on the far enemy.

For the purpose of our analysis, we are going to focus specifically on al-Qaeda's strategy vis-à-vis the United States, fully recognizing that this may be part of a larger grand strategy involving fomenting instability of the Arab states and ultimately the creation of a new Caliphate. We are also going to assume that the goals al-Qaeda established for the United States were to inflict the maximum damage possible, and to drive the United States out of the Middle East. We will now examine the terrorist organization's strategies for attaining these goals, using the framework that has been developed earlier in this book.

Al-Qaeda's Strategy in the Dimension of Systems

Let's begin by examining al-Qaeda's indirect strategy against the United States within the systems dimension. Before we can begin to understand this indirect strategy, we need to first look through the lens al-Qaeda used to analyze the leverage of the United States. Since system level strategies aim to shape the leverage dynamics of the opponent indirectly by targeting its external environment, it is important to tease out how al-Qaeda interpreted the superpower in the context of the international system.

The arc of al-Qaeda's worldview onto the international system extends back to the period preceding the fall of the Ottoman Empire, the subsequent exploitation of the remnants of that Empire by the British and the French, and the creation of artificial states in the Middle East, whose borders were demarcated to serve the imperial interests of the European colonial powers and later served the interests of the United States and Soviet Union. While for al-Qaeda the Ottoman Empire in many ways represented the glory days of Islam, its strategy was largely built on a view of how the United States, as well as the Soviet Union, exerted power over the Middle East during the Cold War. The view was that the two superpowers and their respective satellite states in the Middle East served as an inner core of the international system, with the United Nations representing those countries' interests and providing an outer core of pseudo-legitimacy within that system. This system helped sustain an oppressive status quo for the peoples of the region, and al-Qaeda viewed this structure as perpetuating the superpowers' leverage over the region's more dependent Islamic states.[7]

In al-Qaeda's worldview the militant Islamic movement, and not the U.S. containment strategy, was responsible for the end of the Cold War. It believes that the mujahidin resistance movement in Afghanistan, which continuously drew in increasing numbers of Soviet troops, encouraged the Islamic Soviet Republics to secede and ultimately weakened the Soviet Union to the precipice of collapse.[8] But al-Qaeda's worldview extends beyond this. According to it, the power structure that survived the collapse of the Soviet Union fell under the hegemonic sway of the United States, its regional allies including Israel, and the United Nations. This worldview served as the backdrop for al-Qaeda's strategy.

Al-Qaeda's Strategy of
Disrupting Relationships within the System

In chapter 3 we discussed that an opponent can derive leverage from its external systems environment through relationships it forms, system properties it benefits from, or its position within the system. According to al-Qaeda's worldview, the United States derived leverage from its multiple relationships in the international system. It was the political, military, and economic relationships the United States had forged with Saudi Arabia and other oil producing states in the region that sustained the superpower's reach into the Middle East and beyond. U.S. leverage was also perpetuated by its relationships with non-oil producing states, like Egypt and Jordan. Military and political support for Israel and the fealty of conservative Arab states empowered the United States to battle the more progressive forces of Islam from a safe distance. In other words, because of the relationships the United States had cultivated in the region it had the leverage to sustain the status quo, keeping the lid on the simmering ambitions of the Islamic peoples, with little cost or risk to itself.

In addition to the support provided by Arab countries, al-Qaeda also observed that the United States derived leverage from its alliances with Western European states like Britain, France, and Spain. These countries gave the United States political cover for its hegemonic designs, and support in multilateral forums like the United Nations. They also had their own political and economic interests in, and ambitions for, the Muslim lands of the Middle East.

One key tenet of al-Qaeda's strategy was to disrupt the relationships the United States had established with its Arab allies, particularly oil giant Saudi Arabia. According to al-Qaeda's way of thinking, breaking this link between the Arab countries and the United States would deprive these states of the leverage derived from the superpower, and vice versa.

One way to think about this is that al-Qaeda saw its attacks on the United States (the far enemy) as a means toward liberation of the Arab lands (the near enemy). Al-Qaeda's leaders believed that the key to destabilizing the Arab states was to attack and weaken their benefactor, the United States.[9] As Osama bin-Laden was said to have remarked, "If we cut off the head of America, the kingdoms in the Arab world will cease to exist."[10] He meant that by injuring or crippling the United States, all the leverage Saudi Arabia and other Arab states derive from their relationships with their external systems will dissipate, ultimately contributing to their weakening and eventual collapse.

In addition to weakening Arab states, the strategy also was designed to weaken the United States. Al-Qaeda's support for local Islamic insurgencies in Arab states was designed to put pressure on, and raise the risk for, regimes that backed the United States.[11] The idea was to make any regime the terrorist group saw as beholden to the United States more reluctant to follow a U.S. agenda. Al-Qaeda also understood the importance of oil imports from the Gulf to the United States. Attacks on Saudi Arabia could lead to a spike in oil prices, or an interruption in supply, either of which could put a crimp in the U.S. economy. The terror attacks in Saudi Arabia by al-Qaeda could be interpreted in this light.[12] Although the terrorist organization saw the liberation of Saudi Arabia as part of its master plan, its attacks on this key regional ally of the United States was part of a strategy of indirectly putting pressure on the superpower.[13]

Attacks on U.S. European allies were another piece of al-Qaeda's strategy to compromise the leverage the United States enjoys from its relationships in the international system. The terrorist attacks on the subway systems in Madrid in 2004 and London in 2005 were part of a strategy to drive a wedge between the United States and some of its closest allies.[14] While each of these acts was justified by al-Qaeda on the basis of the behavior of the governments of Spain and the United Kingdom, the goal was to make these countries less supportive of the military adventures initiated by the United States in Iraq and Afghanistan. In fact, this aim was effective in Spain, where shortly after the 2004 subway bombings, the government withdrew its remaining fourteen hundred troops from Afghanistan. Aside from depriving the United States of much needed military assistance, al-Qaeda's strategy was also designed to compromise U.S. leverage by making its allies more circumspect in their diplomatic support for the United States.

Al-Qaeda's Strategy of Creating
Its Own Relationships within the System

Clearly al-Qaeda understood that it could not expect to challenge a superpower with global reach like the United States alone. So it forged relationships and alliances with other groups that could amplify its effectiveness and counteract to some degree the relationships the United States had benefited from. While this activity accelerated after 9/11, the strategy was in place before that event. Al-Qaeda adapted to the international and regional systems by forging alliances across boundaries, craftily adjusting its global narrative to fit the more limited narratives and grievances of local groups. Its relationships with the Egyptian Islamic Jihad, Pakistani Lashkar-e-Taiba, al-Qaeda in the Islamic Maghreb, and the Libyan Islamic Fighting Group, gave it the regional reach it needed to challenge U.S. allies in the region. These alliances enabled al-Qaeda to put further pressure on Middle Eastern regimes and others aligned with the United States.

The brilliance of this strategy came about through al-Qaeda's agility, pragmatism, and flexibility—characteristics not normally attributed to earlier terrorist organizations. While al-Qaeda's leadership controlled its grand strategy and its overarching narrative, it gave operational and ideological latitude to local groups. Each of these groups had their own particular grievances against local regimes, the United States, and Israel, but al-Qaeda's overarching narrative of global oppression overlay nicely with these narratives. While the overlap might not have been 100 percent, there was enough elasticity and flexibility built into the relationship to keep it functioning despite differences in immediate aims.[15]

Al-Qaeda's Strategy of Exploiting Properties of the System

While the United States may have benefited from its position within a globalized international system, al-Qaeda exploited some of the properties of this system, turning what had been a historic advantage for the United States into a distinct liability. The system properties al-Qaeda exploited were sovereignty gaps within the international system. These gaps were created by fragile or failed states that lacked control over their territories, like Somalia, Yemen, loosely governed areas of Pakistan, and pre-9/11 Afghanistan. These were and still are states beset by internecine strife, weak central governments, and an inability to exert control over their borders. In an international system that functioned largely according to principles of state sovereignty, these governance voids created strategic opportunities for al-Qaeda. Despite relatively meager resources, al-Qaeda took advantage of these gaps to increase its own capacity. These countries gave al-Qaeda the geographic space and freedom of movement it needed to battle the United States and its regional proxies. The relationships with these fragile or failed countries gave al-Qaeda leverage by giving them the protection of the state, along with the ability to establish its own independent operational base from which to attack and challenge the United States. Al-Qaeda set up bases, training centers, and relationships with local governments, giving it the freedom to conduct operations, without any accountability.

In some cases these countries became safe havens and operational bases for al-Qaeda by default and in others by design. In Afghanistan al-Qaeda was given a safe haven by design, with the radical Taliban rulers welcoming and collaborating with the terrorist group. In Yemen al-Qaeda benefited more by default, with large parts of the country outside the security reach of former president Ali Abdullah Saleh. These ungoverned areas of Yemen served, and continue to serve, as prime operational real estate for al-Qaeda.

So let's briefly summarize al-Qaeda's system level strategy for dealing with the United States. One of the strategies this terrorist organization used was to reduce the leverage the United States received from its allies. Using alliances with local jihadist groups, it put pressure on Arab regimes and held them accountable for their alliances with the United States. Particularly with Saudi Arabia, al-Qaeda targeted a regime that not only provided political support for the United States, but also served as the major supplier of oil to the West. Moreover, al-Qaeda tried to disrupt the united front the United States had forged with its European allies. In addition to strategies aimed at attenuating the power of the United States, al-Qaeda also used strategies to improve its own leverage position. Its support for local opposition movements and its exploitation of fragile states gave it a capability that was disproportionately larger than its resources.

Al-Qaeda's Strategy in the Dimension of Opponents

In addition to indirect strategies, al-Qaeda also unleashed a set of direct strategies at the United States. Remember that direct strategies work through a couple of different types of mechanisms. We will see that al-Qaeda saw the acts of 9/11 as attenuating U.S. capability, potentially shifting the motivation of the U.S. government and public, and as disrupting the U.S. strategy. Let's look at how the terrorist group developed these strategies aimed directly at the United States.

Al-Qaeda's Strategy for Compromising
the Capability of the United States

While al-Qaeda has made some miscalculations about the resiliency and will of the United States, its analysis of U.S. capability is quite accurate and gives us a window onto its strategic thinking going into 9/11. While al-Qaeda underestimated the resolve of the United States, it had few illusions about, and in fact, had a healthy respect for, its raw capability. It never envisioned decisively defeating the United States militarily on the battlefield or through direct attack. It clearly understood that the United States had significant military and technological advantages that couldn't be overcome.

But al-Qaeda's view of the United States' other capabilities is the most revealing and important for an understanding of their strategy. They viewed the other main pillars of strength to be the U.S. economic system, its institutions, and its national will.[16] It was these non-military capabilities that they saw as vulnerable, and which became the centerpiece of al-Qaeda's strategy of direct confrontation.

More specifically, al-Qaeda saw the economic system as the linchpin of U.S. capability, meaning its military, national will and other capabilities flowed from the strength of the capitalist system. While the health of the U.S. economic engine translated into military and political might, al-Qaeda also believed it created certain vulnerabilities. Thus, economic capability became the focal point of al-Qaeda's strategy in the dimension of the opponent.

What follows are some of the particulars of al-Qaeda's strategy targeting the capability of the United States. The first was that a successful attack on September 11, 2001, would significantly weaken the U.S. economy, the linchpin of the superpower's capability. Their belief was that attacks on the twin towers of the World Trade Center in New York, as well as on the Pentagon and White House in Washington, D.C., would roil financial markets and produce a destabilizing effect on the U.S. economy. By doing this, al-Qaeda hoped to bring about the eventual contraction of U.S. military capability and weaken the will of the American people.[17]

But there was a second and more indirect way the attacks of 9/11 were designed to cripple U.S. capability. It involved baiting the United

States to take actions that would place it in a strategically vulnerable and indefensible position. Al-Qaeda believed that while attacks on U.S. soil, like those of 9/11, could injure the United States, the only way to defeat or cripple the superpower was to lure it into battles in the Middle East and Afghanistan. The attacks were designed to provoke the United States into retaliating against Afghanistan using its military might. Once the United States entered the inhospitable topographic and ethnic terrain of that country, its forces would get mired in an untenable, unwinnable, and ultimately enervating situation. This would bleed the U.S. military, but also put strains on its economy, the linchpin of its overall capability.

Al-Qaeda had a historic reference point for their strategy once the United States invaded Afghanistan, which was the experience of Islamic mujahidin guerillas driving out the Soviets from Afghanistan in the 1980s. Al-Qaeda believed that like the Soviets, the United States would bleed to death when forced to fight Islamic forces in the treacherous mountains of Afghanistan.[18] They were convinced that if the Soviets had lost, U.S. forces, which they saw as far less ruthless, would meet an even quicker and more treacherous demise.[19]

Could one take a contrary view and reasonably argue that al-Qaeda hadn't expected the United States to target Afghanistan, and only with the benefit of hindsight did they claim this as their strategy? The record seems unsupportive of this argument. In addition to written documents, al-Qaeda's actions in the days leading up to 9/11 point to the fact that they fully intended the United States to respond in the way it did. In retrospect, the assassination of Northern Alliance leader Ahmad Shah Massoud a few days before 9/11 was one of the tell-tale signs. It was known that the Northern Alliance was the only formidable opponent to the Taliban and al-Qaeda in Afghanistan. Al-Qaeda believed that decapitating the leadership of the Northern Alliance would hobble it and make it a less effective partner for the United States, who, after being attacked, would become determined to dislodge the Taliban. Moreover, they believed that killing Massoud would make the Taliban beholden to al-Qaeda, thus making it more difficult for the United States to drive a wedge between Taliban leader Mullah Omar and Osama bin Laden.[20]

Al-Qaeda's Strategy for Shifting the
Motivation and Will of the United States

Al-Qaeda believed that several things motivated the foreign policy of the United States. It appears that al-Qaeda evaluated U.S. core interests to be preserving and fueling the country's dynamic economic system, maintaining hegemonic control over the Middle East, and maintaining Israel's security. As far as the U.S. perception of threat and opportunity, al-Qaeda seemed to conclude that with the end of the Cold War, the demise of the Soviet Union, and with no single opponent on the horizon, the United States perceived mostly opportunity to advance its interests.

Al-Qaeda's strategy was designed to reduce the motivation of the United States to stay committed to the Middle East. The idea was that a protracted war in Afghanistan would sap the will of the American people to fight and reduce their appetite for foreign adventures in the Middle East. Unlike the Soviets, whose war adventures didn't need popular support to be sustained, U.S. war fighting capability was dependent on the American people. Al-Qaeda's strategy was to exhaust the U.S. military, bleed it economically, and sap the motivation of the American people.[21]

Disrupting the Strategy of the United States

Though it is not clear exactly how al-Qaeda interpreted the strategy of the United States, we can infer some conclusions from their writings. First, al-Qaeda could have concluded that before 9/11 the United States lacked a strategy for defeating terrorism. While there had been some individual retaliatory responses to terrorist attacks against U.S. interests, there was clearly no overarching strategy. Second, al-Qaeda observed that the United States was able to perpetuate its interests in the region through an indirect strategy rather than through direct conflict. Its strategy was to work through local Arab proxies and Israel, without the need to put much of its own skin in the game.

Al-Qaeda's actions were designed to force the United States into a direct fight against an opponent and raise the costs of its strategy of pursuing regional interests through alignments with conservative Arab regimes and Israel. No longer would the United States be able to pursue its interests without taking significant risk.[22] While support for Arab regimes and Israel contributed to the leverage the United States enjoyed, al-Qaeda's attacks would in effect drive up the price of sustaining these alliances, ultimately making the costs unacceptable. This would in effect force the United States to reprioritize its interests and change its policies.

So let's review al-Qaeda's strategy at the level of the opponent. There were several different strands. The first was that the strategy of 9/11 was designed to disrupt the capability of the United States by weakening the linchpin of its capability—the economy. This event was also designed to neutralize the capability of the United States by luring it into Afghanistan and into a position of overextension. Like the Soviets during the Cold War, the United States would become ensnared in a trap set by al-Qaeda and the Taliban. Al-Qaeda's strategy was also designed to alter the motivation of the United States by pushing it from a position of opportunity to a posture of threat. The corollary to this would be that the United States would recalibrate its interests with respect to its Arab allies. Finally, al-Qaeda wanted to disrupt U.S. strategy by forcing it away from the strategy of pursuing its interests through alliances and toward a strategy of a direct, deadly engagement.

Al-Qaeda's Strategy in the Dimension of Groups

Because of al-Qaeda's underdog status, it needed to create a multiplier effect on its resources. Strategy in the dimension of groups was an integral part of its strategy for doing this; it mobilized groups in the Middle East, Europe, and the United States that could augment its efforts. Al-Qaeda built alliances with like-minded groups in countries with fragile governments and limited sovereignty, like Algeria, Sudan, Yemen, and Pakistan. These groups, including al-Shabaab in Somalia, al-Qaeda in the Arabian Peninsula, and the Taliban, gave al-Qaeda the ability to project power and secure safe havens and bases in the interstices of the international system. The idea was to foment instability where there was stability, and where there was already instability, use it to the terrorist group's advantage. Al-Qaeda used other types of formal groups to enhance its position and fuel its sustainability, like using Islamic charities and NGOs to raise money and help sustain its operations.[23]

But one of the most potent parts of al-Qaeda's strategy focused on more informal groups. Al-Qaeda projected influence by mobilizing different groups of constituencies in the region, in effect sucking the oxygen out of the U.S. public diplomacy strategy designed to improve the reputation of the United States among the Muslim masses. In order to build regional support for its narrative among these groups, al-Qaeda leveraged the Internet to its advantage.

A Strategy of Targeting Specific Groups

In order to understand al-Qaeda's strategy for groups, we need to look at who they were targeting, what methods they were using, and what their aims for the group were. Al-Qaeda broke target audiences into groups, analogous to the way a consumer products company targets market segments. They sliced and diced their target audiences into segments and sub-segments, depending on the message and aim they had for the group. The most all-encompassing group was the broader Islamic community. Since al-Qaeda's ultimate aspiration was to create a new Caliphate on the lines of the former Ottoman Empire, connecting to and mobilizing the Islamic masses was an important part of its strategy. This large target audience was then further dichotomized into groups that were part of the near enemy and groups that were part of the far enemy.[24] The near enemy consisted of populations in conservative Arab countries governed by rulers whose interests are tied to the west. The far enemy consisted of populations living in the United States and Europe.

But al-Qaeda went even further, breaking the masses down into more refined and particular demographic segments. Sometimes al-Qaeda broke its target audiences down by country, such as the Iraqi people or the Muslim Brothers in Somalia.[25] Other times it broke its audiences down by type of grievance, such as the Pakistanis who longed for Kashmir, or the Palestinians who longed for an independent state.[26]

The sub-segmentation strategy was also used with populations in the far enemy countries. Within those countries were a couple different target audiences. One was the diaspora Muslim communities residing in the West. These were audiences that might be sympathetic to the narrative propagated by al-Qaeda, and who could potentially be mobilized against their host governments. The other audience was the non-Muslim masses in far enemy countries. While it is unlikely that this group could be ever turned against their own government, the goal was to sow disillusionment with their government's foreign policy positions.[27]

In order to reach these target audiences, al-Qaeda customized their messaging strategy by dividing target audiences into sub-segments based on the goals at hand. For example, al-Qaeda targeted specific segments of populations in the Middle East and the West on behalf of the goal of recruitment. They then used sophisticated market segmentation methods to break down these populations into sub-segments such as hardcore jihadist activists and less radicalized jihadist potentials. While the former might be reached through radicalized imams, the latter might be reached using the Internet or other alternative media. Other methods would target specific sub-segments of these groups for fund-raising purposes. Each audience would be reached by a particular method and with a customized message which was tailored for maximum effectiveness and impact.[28]

Ideological narratives were another method al-Qaeda used to mobilize their various audiences.[29] While there were a number of different themes, one of the universal narratives involved the grievances Palestinians had with Israel.[30] Regardless of the country, this message seemed to resonate with virtually all audiences, and it was, and still is, part of a strategy to put pressure on the United States, as it ties the existence of Israel, and its actions, to what al-Qaeda portrays as U.S. hegemonic interests. Other themes were that the United States was an effete, weakening power that was stealing Muslim oil. The idea was to use overarching narratives, like the Israel-Palestine message, on all audiences but then customize other messages for particular audiences, such as the Pakistanis, Iraqis, and other peoples with particular grievances or ambitions. Al-Qaeda also used very sophisticated timing to its advantage. It used particular messages around anniversaries of previous terrorist attacks and transmitted tailored messages to mobilize support right before and right after fresh attacks.

From what we can discern from al-Qaeda's pronouncements, their aims, which are the specific behaviors the strategy is designed to elicit, varied by target audience. For example converting inert, indolent masses into active jihadists would be one aim of the messages geared to Pakistanis living in the United Kingdom, while general recruitment may have been the aim in Somalia. For the broader Islamic audiences, the aim was to legitimize the terrorist group and mobilize opposition to corrupt regimes. One of al-Qaeda's aims for its audiences in the United States was sowing public dissent to the government's policies in the Middle East. To do this they played on racial and partisan tensions, casting aspersions on U.S. policies in the region. Again the aim was to undermine popular support for the country's foreign policy.[31]

Al-Qaeda's Group Strategy post-9/11

While it is impossible to precisely gauge the success of al-Qaeda's strategies aimed at informal groups, it is clear that they have been successful in framing and communicating their narrative in the Middle East. Despite significant public diplomacy efforts by the United States, al-Qaeda's methods have reinforced the sentiment that the superpower is an aggressor with hegemonic designs. How this will translate into significant benefits for the terrorist group in the future is uncertain. But what we can conclude is that up until now the United States has been on the losing side of the war of ideas.[32]

A natural follow-on question is what is the significance of the Arab Spring for al-Qaeda's strategy? If the upending of the status quo in the Arab world is occurring with little or no contribution from al-Qaeda, what does this mean for its carefully cultivated narrative?

The events taking place in the Arab world may actually constitute a strategic threat to al-Qaeda for several reasons. The first is that in most countries the secular or more reformist Islamic groups, not the religious zealots, fomented the instability. Mohamed Morsi from the Muslim Brotherhood, who won the presidency in Egypt, will be challenged by these secular-minded groups that are sensitive to the perception that the Egyptian rebellion has been hijacked by Islamic radicals. Moreover, economic imperatives in Egypt will likely prevent Morsi from running completely afoul of the West. Because of these factors, it is highly unlikely the rise of a leader from an Islamic group will translate into gains for al-Qaeda or move the region closer to the terrorist group's aspiration of Islamic unity. Second, while al-Qaeda spokespersons publicly supported the protests taking place in these Arab countries, it seems quite plausible that these transformations could threaten the legitimacy and resonance of the terrorist group's narrative.[33] The exception may be in Yemen, where further erosion in the state's power may actually lead to gains on the part of al-Qaeda in the Arabian Peninsula, and possibly Syria, where al-Qaeda and other groups could take advantage of a downward spiral toward civil war and a loss of control by the government. Third, while al-Qaeda preaches that political changes can only occur through violence, the initial phase of the transformations in Tunisia and Egypt occurred relatively peacefully.

Does al-Qaeda's loss of control of their narrative necessarily mean a corresponding win for the United States? While answers to this question are elusive, one could argue that the events in the Arab world, and the concomitant dilution of al-Qaeda's narrative, present an opportunity for the United States. If the country is perceived as being supportive of the forces for change, then it is possible that the United States could gain the initiative in the war of ideas against radical voices like al-Qaeda. But if the actions and words of the United States are perceived as backing the entrenched regimes in Bahrain and Yemen, then the old impressions of the past may be reinforced. The trick will be to balance the traditional interests the United States has had with regimes in Yemen and Bahrain with new regional interests that will emerge out of the transformed political landscape of the Arab Spring.

Does al-Qaeda Get the Power of Integration?

So how does strategy in 3D work for al-Qaeda? Do the system, opponent, and group strategies reinforce one another in a formulaic fashion, or are the different components completely independent? Does strategic success necessitate traction at all three levels, or can success take place with traction in just two or even one of the dimensions? Has al-Qaeda derived a multiplier effect from the different pieces of its strategy?

It seems reasonably clear that al-Qaeda's strategies in the three dimensions were formulaic, as they did mutually reinforce one another. Without safe havens in fragile states (systems strategy) it is unlikely that al-Qaeda could have orchestrated the massive 9/11 attack on U.S. soil and continued to operate in the aftermath. Without the ability to recruit from Islamic communities (group strategy) it would be difficult for a single terrorist organization to mount such an aggressive attack on U.S. global interests. There was also the strategy of luring the United States into Afghanistan (opponent strategy). As economically damaging as the 9/11 attacks were, it pales in comparison with the economic cost of the subsequent wars in both Afghanistan and Iraq. Direct attacks were designed to hobble the United States, while the indirect strategies were designed to keep the country on the defensive. These strategies were designed to threaten U.S. alliances and build anti-American sentiment across the Middle East, which would impair the United States' ability to project power in the region.

In terms of whether al-Qaeda's strategy created a multiplier effect, we need to address the question of whether its strategy brought it any closer to its goals. In other words, aside from the operational successes they have enjoyed, how does their strategy measure up? Given that twelve years after invading Afghanistan the United States is still mired in conflict and the U.S. economy is still anemic, it may be that al-Qaeda could reasonably claim to have achieved its goal of weakening the U.S. economy. But against the broader goal of getting the United States to disengage from the region, success has been more elusive. Even though we have withdrawn troops from Iraq, and are likely to do the same in Afghanistan in 2014, there is still a strong sentiment in the United States to support Israel and the commitment to the Persian Gulf countries seems still resolute.

How do al-Qaeda's successes measure up against its grand strategy aspiration of awakening the Islamic masses and forming a new Islamic Caliphate? This goal, if ever realizable, seems remote within the context of the events unfolding with the Arab Spring. It is unlikely that al-Qaeda or any of its affiliates will ever gain the upper hand in most of these countries, notwithstanding the gains they may make in places like Somalia and Yemen. While they still persist in their role of destabilizing the status quo, al-Qaeda doesn't seem likely to be able to channel this into creating a new future order.

But, is the failure to advance towards the goal of forming a new Islamic Caliphate strategically important for al-Qaeda? Is acting as an agent of instability enough? If al-Qaeda fit the model of previous terrorist groups, the answer to the last question might be yes. But al-Qaeda is a new breed of terrorist organization, both in the scope of its operations and the sophistication of its strategic thinking. For al-Qaeda, terrorist raids and attacks are means to an end, not ends in themselves. So if attacks don't lead to an ultimate retreat of the United States from the region, and don't result in the replacement of conservative Arab regimes with militant Islamic leaders, then they have failed strategically. Al-Qaeda may reconstitute itself in the wake of the assassination of Osama bin Laden, refocusing its efforts on Pakistan and Afghanistan and somehow trying to regain the initiative lost as the result of the Arab Spring, but it still seems unlikely that it will advance much closer to its broad strategic goals.

But while al-Qaeda may have overreached in terms of the goals it set out for itself, it would be unwise to consider it a complete strategic failure. If we recast the goals to be the disruption of U.S. strategy, then the terrorist organization might be considered more of a strategic success. Along with the Taliban, al-Qaeda has forestalled U.S. attempts to create sustainable stability in Afghanistan. Moreover, the United States is clearly in a weaker economic position than any time in its history. While much of this has come about as a result of the financial crisis of 2007–2008, and subsequent problems in the Euro zone, one should not discount the negative economic impact of two costly wars. Given al-Qaeda's strategy of luring the United States into Afghanistan and bleeding it, one cannot fail to be struck by their success in this area. Not only has this war, along with the war in Iraq, been costly in terms of lives, it has also contributed to the budget deficit and the economic problems the United States is confronting today. What impact this will have on future U.S. policy in the Middle East is still unclear. But what is clear is that it will force us to reframe our options, something that can be directly attributable to al-Qaeda's successes.

What Does This Mean for a Counterterrorism Strategy?

So what does a 3D understanding of al-Qaeda's strategy reveal to us about a possible U.S. counterterrorism strategy? It suggests that the strategy needs to take into account all three dimensions of the strategic environment. Killing Osama bin Laden and other al-Qaeda leaders, an example of an opponent strategy, was, and still is, important in hobbling the terrorist group. But the other dimensions of strategy are also critical. While direct attacks on the terrorist organization may be imperative, equally important are system strategies aimed at countering al-Qaeda's attempts to expand the number of safe havens around the globe. Al-Qaeda survives because persistent weaknesses and gaps in the international system allow it to establish a global footprint with bases of operations. But this requires that weak or failing states be complicit, or at least acquiescent, to terrorist groups.[34] System strategies that focus on building capacity in fragile states like Somalia, Yemen, and Mali, and efforts that focus on changing the incentives of states aligned with al-Qaeda, would severely hobble the terrorist organization. Moreover, a more robust public diplomacy group strategy could also be instrumental in countering the war of ideas that al-Qaeda has launched. A war of negatives might be even more effective than a strategy of extolling the virtues of the United States. This public diplomacy campaign would focus on the excesses of al-Qaeda, such as the use of violence against Muslims, as being un-Islamic.[35] Whether al-Qaeda can be completely defeated is unclear. But what is clear is that any effective counter-strategy needs to encompass all three dimensions of the strategic environment.

CONCLUSION:
STRATEGIC THINKING IN 3D

N ever has there been a time in our history when the need for strategic thinking and effective strategy has been greater than it is today. The magnitude of the economic and national security problems we face makes strategic thinking and strategic institutional capacity absolute imperatives. But at a time when the demand for strategic capacity has increased, the supply has not. Our governing institutions, both in the public and private sectors, seem to operate on, and according to, short-term time horizons. The complexity of the world we live in, coupled with the fire-hose-like deluge of information flowing to policymakers and stewards of industry, crowds out the ability to think beyond the immediate. Even leaders who are naturally predisposed to longer-term strategic thinking find that the crush of short-term realities, and the lack of institutional reinforcement, make holding on to a longer-term strategic view difficult if not impossible.

While part of the problem stems from institutional capacity issues, another contributor is the apparent loss of an appreciation for the art and science of strategy. Strategy is about making possible what otherwise might be improbable. It is about adapting to or shaping an organization's external environment on behalf of its goals. Strategy is about creating and then exploiting leverage over an opponent or problem. Finally strategy is about generating energy and creating a multiplier effect on resources and actions. We need a framework that helps the practitioner appreciate and embrace strategy as an energetic discipline that captures these dynamics.

This book attempts to make the case, and provide one method, for reclaiming strategy as an approachable and practicable discipline. It is for the professional who wants to start thinking strategically but doesn't have a frame of reference or starting point. It is for government leaders who need to grapple with the strategic problems facing their country, but also want to comprehend the strategic circumstances of current or potential adversaries. The book is also relevant to business leaders who need a framework for understanding their company's strategic environment, as well the outlook of competitors, potential partners, and governments. And finally it is for anyone who wants to become a consummate strategist, better able to analyze and cope with the complexity of problems that exist outside the walls of their own organizations.

So what does it take for people to begin to think strategically? More than likely if they are positioned at the senior ranks of any organization, they already have most, if not all, of the basics. Thinking about strategic environments is something they probably already do. But a more disciplined, methodical way to think about these environments can help elevate the strategic thinking skills of a seasoned professional.

This book has portrayed strategy as having both an inward and outward face based on the idea that strategists have to focus their thoughts and actions both inside and outside an organization or country. The inward face of strategy involves setting goals and manufacturing capability. But in order for strategic traction to take place, the energetic muscular capability created internally needs to be applied to an organization's external environment, where ultimate strategic success or failure is determined. This external environment is the outward face of strategy.

The outward face of strategy involves operating in a 3D environment, consisting of the dimensions of systems, opponents, and groups. While time constraints often force the strategist to deal with these different dimensions simultaneously, this book has treated them individually. Although there is something artificial about disaggregating strategy in this way, it is important to consider each of these different dimensions separately before integrating them. This will sensitize the strategist to the particular and unique challenges of using strategy in each dimension.

Studying these different dimensions individually, however, doesn't obviate the need to eventually consider them together. It is by focusing on the three dimensions of strategy together that the power of integration and the resultant multiplier effects can be realized. Although it is true that goals can sometimes be achieved without hitting home runs in all of these dimensions, the competent strategist is wise to consider options in all three. Moreover, focusing on all three dimensions of strategy will lessen the likelihood of miscalculation or the omission of something important.

What follows will summarize the main lessons and key insights about the inward and outward faces of strategy that the strategist should glean from this book. These guidelines should help the strategist better and more methodically evaluate options within each of the different dimensions of strategic reality.

THE INWARD FACE OF STRATEGY

The inward face of strategy involves creating the internal energy and muscle needed for the outward face of strategy. This involves the setting of goals and the marshalling of resources on behalf of creating capability.

Goals shouldn't be set in a vacuum
Goals need to be derived from the interests of the country or organization. Core interests are what need to be protected or improved for the health of the organization or country, while situational interests are what are at stake in a particular situation or conflict. Goals need to reinforce or protect these core and situational interests. If the goals of your strategy are disconnected from, or in conflict with, the interests of your organization, you may be able to claim tactical success but could very well experience strategic failure.

Set primary, subsidiary, and milestone goals
Primary goals may be general and not conducive to measurement or management. If this is the case, be sure to set subsidiary goals, which are more measurable, granular expressions of primary goals. For goals cast far into the future, ground your strategy by setting intermediate milestones, which indicate progress on the way toward the fulfillment of the primary goals.

Focus first on capability, then resources
Having access to appropriate and sufficient resources is critical to the success of any strategy. But many times the process of budgeting for and

allocating resources is wrongly mistaken for strategy. Mistaking resource allocation for strategy is the equivalent of receiving five hundred electronic parts in a box and calling it a computer. Until the parts are connected, assembled, and wired, there is no computer. The same is true with strategy. Until inert assets are connected and leveraged to create muscular capability, there is no strategy.

Manufacturing capability is one of the most critical parts of strategy. Think of capability as the organizational equivalent of a finely tuned muscle that makes particular types of motion and action possible. Even when not fully flexed, the capabilities of an organization give it the potential to act.

THE OUTWARD FACE OF STRATEGY

While the energy of strategy in the form of capability gets created as part of the inward face of strategy, its deployment and transmission into the external environment represent the outward face of strategy.

Strategy in the Dimension of Systems

Why is strategy in the dimension of systems important? Competitive strategy necessitates an understanding of how your opponents derive leverage from their external environment and how they are connected with other actors in this environment. In addition, opponents may derive leverage from webs of formal and informal connections between actors, institutions, and processes in the system, not just from individual, bilateral relationships. Developing a strategy to cripple an opponent requires an understanding of how these connections work, and how the opponent is positioned within the system. Understanding this gives the strategist insights into ways to disrupt the leverage that comes from these systems.

It is important to remember that system level strategy is a form of indirect strategy, as it is aimed not at the opponent directly, but at its environment. This type of strategy may be a way to deal a blow to the adversary without a direct confrontation, or if a confrontation is necessary, it may be a way to soften the environment so that the fight is decisively in your favor. Strategy is also about exploiting leverage, which can be created by either improving your own position or denigrating your opponent's standing. Since leverage can come from the opponent's relationships with others, the properties of the system, or the opponent's position within the system, the strategist should be focused on how to disrupt these connections and advantages. The greater degree to which you can improve you own position within the system, not just disrupt the opponent's, the greater the chance you will have created a substantial and sustainable leverage position.

Strategy in the Dimension of Opponents

While not all problems involve an adversary, any strategist should be prepared for the possibility that their plans will be challenged by an opponent. There are some specific ways to think about prevailing over, or influencing the behavior of, an opponent. The first is to attack the opponent's capability, blocking its ability to carry out its strategy or to respond to yours. This involves disrupting the opponent's core linchpin capability, such that it is weakened. The second way is to dissuade the adversary from exercising the capability it has. That is if disrupting the opponent's capability isn't feasible or prudent, the strategist should be thinking about ways to motivate it to alter its plans. Focusing on the motivation of the opponent as opposed to its capability involves thinking about how to change the way the opponent thinks about its interests and its risk calculus. The third way is to counter the opponent's strategy. If you can't compromise the opponent's capability to pursue its strategy, or dissuade it from a particular action, disrupting its strategy is another way to prevail.

But the strategist should never lose sight of the fact that strategy in the dimension of opponents involves the art of the maneuver. This means that launching your strategy will likely cause a reaction from the adversary, which will then necessitate a counter-reaction from you. And since it is impossible to completely predict the opponent's response once your opening gambit is made, strategy in this dimension will likely be adapted on the fly. This also puts a finer point on the value of system strategies, where not every move produces a reaction from the opponent.

Strategy in the Dimension of Groups

Strategy in the dimension of groups is a partly a phenomenon of the world in which we live today. Consumers and citizens have the potential to organize challenges to authority in ways that were unimaginable even twenty years ago. The ability for consumers and non-profits to challenge the reputation of a business is greater today than ever before. And, as is evidenced by the Arab Spring, citizen groups have the ability to challenge the legitimacy of states, regimes, and leaders. The strategist who ignores this dimension of strategy does so at their peril.

Like system strategies, strategy in the dimension of groups is an indirect form of strategy. While strategy in this dimension may provoke a response from the adversary, it is not aimed directly at them. It can involve formal groups that have established structure, or informal groups that lack any formal structure. It is important to remember that groups can come in all shapes and sizes. Informal groups can be inchoate, emerging entities like the Tea Party, or completely unorganized collections of individuals like consumer market or voter segments. Formal groups can be hierarchical and long-standing, or more fleeting like the G20, which for the most part only exists when the member states convene. It is also important to decide how you are going to influence the behavior of the group. Are you going to use carrots, sticks, or a combination of both to motivate the group to move in the direction you desire? The strategist needs to articulate how influencing the behavior of the group is going to affect the leverage of the opponent. Finally, the strategist needs to understand how this leverage will actually influence the behavior of the opponent.

FINAL THOUGHTS ON STRATEGY

Up to this point, thinking like a strategist seems pretty straightforward. All the strategist needs to do is follow the steps of analyzing each of the dimensions of the strategic environment, and then consider strategic options within those dimensions. If only strategy were so easy. While the frame presented gives the strategist a method for thinking strategically, prevailing in the game of strategy isn't quite so easy.

First, success depends on analyzing and acting in all three dimensions of the strategic environment simultaneously. While each dimension has been treated separately, in the real worlds of business, foreign policy, and national security, reality is messy and chaotic and defies any overly sequenced approach to strategy. While it may be desirable to first reduce the leverage of the adversary through indirect system or group strategies before confronting the opponent directly, these types of strategy may be conflated under the weight of situational realities. Second, the strategist may put in an immense amount of analysis and planning, only to be forced to deviate from, or more likely revise, their strategies on the fly. All of the forethought and planning in the world may go out the window under the crush of the enemy's reaction to your opening move. The third is the complexity of the strategic realities we face today. As much as a U.S. strategist can try to understand the strategic reality of the rise of China, the complexities and pace of its rise may defy a clear strategic analysis. And while it is critical that we develop strategy for complex challenges like this, getting it right is very difficult.

Given these admonishments and caveats, what is the utility of a frame that attempts to organize a reality that may defy organization? Don't we run the risk of lulling the strategist into complacency by suggesting that all that is needed for successful strategies is rigorously following the 3D framework? If the framework is used obtusely like a meat cleaver, rather than subtly and suggestively like a surgeon's scalpel, then the framework may actually be a dangerous tool. But if the framework is used subtly to ask the right questions, rather than dogmatically to provide clear answers, it can be a powerful tool for the strategist. It is best used to structure and stimulate the strategist's thinking, prodding him or her to dig deeper, make more informed decisions, and act and react within the context of a well-defined strategic environment.

Will the use of the framework help close the gap between the demand for strategy and our capacity to make it? It depends. For organizations that understand the value of long-term strategic thinking, the framework can be helpful in creating strategic thinking capacity. It can help sensitize leaders of these organizations to the fact that wins in each of the three dimensions can mutually reinforce one another, creating a compounding or multiplier effect towards the achievement of the goal. But it is no substitute for developing a strategic culture within governments or businesses. No tool can compensate for the shortsightedness of business and government leaders who believe that long-term strategic analysis is a luxury the policymaker can't afford.

The framework presented in this book can be a powerful tool for the enlightened leader who understands the value of strategy, but doesn't know where to begin, by providing guideposts for a process that typically lacks any order. And if it gives business, foreign policy, and national security leaders something that will help them groom future strategists within their own organizations, then I have done the job I have set out to do.

NOTES

PREFACE

1. For the use of the fable of the elephant to describe different view of national security, see Hans Binnendijk and Richard L. Kugler, *Seeing the Elephant: The U.S. Role in Global Security* (Washington, DC: Potomac Books, 2006), xi.
2. For a discussion about how military and political professionals have difficulty communicating on issues relating to strategy, see Colin S. Gray, *Modern Strategy* (New York: Oxford University Press, 1999), 58–68.
3. For a lucid presentation of business strategy, see Michael Porter, *Competitive Strategy: Techniques for Analyzing Industries and Competitors* (New York: Free Press, 1980).
4. For the historical development of business strategy out of military strategy, see Robert M. Grant, *Contemporary Strategy Analysis*, 5th ed. (Malden, MA: Blackwell Publishing, 2005), 14. For a comprehensive analysis of global corporate strategy, see George S. Yip, *Total Global Strategy II: Updated for the Internet and Service Era* (Upper Saddle River, NJ: Prentice Hall, 2003). For an example of how military strategy has been applied to business, see *Clausewitz on Strategy: Inspiration and Insight from a Master Strategist*, eds. Tiha Von Ghyczy, Christopher Bassford, and Bolko von Oetinger (New York: Wiley, 2001).
5. Harry R. Yarger, *Strategy and the National Security Professional: Strategic Thinking and Strategy Formulation in the 21st Century* (Westport, CT: Praeger Security International, 2008), vii–viii.
6. Ibid., 51–53.
7. Colin Gray speaks of strategy as part of human nature in *Modern Strategy*, 358.
8. For the trend toward generals needing to avail themselves of strategies that are outside the lane of traditional military strategy, see Thom Shanker,

"Win Wars? Today's Generals Must Also Politick and Do P.R.," *New York Times*, August 12, 2010.

9. I want to thank Leon Fuerth, former vice president Al Gore's national security advisor, for offering the comparison between different languages with a common root and different types of strategy having common characteristics.

10. For a description of the different levels of strategy, see Edward N. Luttwak, *Strategy: The Logic of War and Peace* (Cambridge, MA: Belknap Press of Harvard University Press, 1987), 69–176. Luttwak also provides a description of the vertical and horizontal dimensions of strategy in *Strategy* (70). For an analysis focusing on the operational and execution side of strategy, see Larry Bossidy and Ram Charan, *Execution: The Discipline of Getting Things Done* (New York: Crown Business, 2002).

INTRODUCTION: DEMYSTIFYING STRATEGY

1. See Richard K. Betts, "Is Strategy an Illusion?," *International Security* 25, no. 2 (Fall 2000): 16. His work calls into question whether strategy in the classic sense can be practiced in a democracy. For an example of another military historian who expounds on why strategy is so difficult, see David Jablonsky, "Why Is Strategy Difficult?," ch. 11 in *U.S. Army War College Guide to Strategy*, eds. Joseph R. Cerami and James F. Holcomb Jr. (Carlisle, PA: U.S. Army War College, 2001).

2. Some of the better literature that operationalizes the concept of strategy in a way that cuts across professions addresses it through the notion of strategic thinking. For a pithy and well-organized work on strategic thinking, see Ken'ichi Ōhmae, *The Mind of the Strategist: The Art of Japanese Business* (New York: McGraw Hill, 1982).

3. For a discussion about how strategy involves the creation of energy, see David S. Evans and Richard Schmalensee, *Catalyst Code: The Strategies Behind the World's Most Dynamic Companies* (Boston: Harvard Business School Press, 2007).

4. Andrew F. Krepinevich and Barry D. Watts, *Regaining Strategic Competence* (Washington, DC: Center for Strategic and Budgetary Assessments, 2009), 19.

5. Arthur F. Lykke Jr., "A Methodology for Developing a Military Strategy," in *Military Strategy: Theory and Application*, ed. Arthur F. Lykke Jr. (Carlisle, PA: U.S. Army War College, 1993). Also for an excellent depiction of Lykke's work, see H. Richard Yarger, "Towards a Theory of Strategy: Art Lykke and the Army War College Strategy Model," in *The U.S. Army War*

College Guide to National Security Issues, 4th ed., ed. J. Boone Bartholomees Jr. (Carlisle, PA: Strategic Studies Institute, 2010), vol. 1, ch. 3.

6. For another portrayal of strategy that implies it is the calibration between ends, ways, and means, see B. H. Liddell Hart, *Strategy* (New York: Praeger, 1954), 336.

7. John Lewis Gaddis, "What is Grand Strategy?" (Karl Von Der Heyden Distinguished Lecture, Duke University, Durham, NC, February 26, 2009), 7 (italics mine). Gaddis's keynote address was for a conference on "American Grand Strategy after War," sponsored by the Triangle Institute for Security Studies and the Duke University Program in American Grand Strategy.

8. For an analysis of how small things can make a big difference, see Malcolm Gladwell, *The Tipping Point: How Little Things Can Make a Big Difference* (Boston: Back Bay Books, 2002). As a subtle contrast to this, see James F. Holcomb, "Managing Strategic Risk," in *Guide to National Security Issues*, Bartholomees, 1:74–75. He argues that though strategy may involve smaller means for larger goals, the risk is much higher. Deriving from Beaufre, he shows different imbalances between means and ends, correlating them to different types of strategy. This is a very useful analysis, as it shows that though strategy may involve outsized goals, there is still needs to be some relationship between means and ends.

9. Betts, "Is Strategy an Illusion?," 6.

10. Kenneth R. Andrews, *The Concept of Corporate Strategy*, 2nd ed. (Homewood, IL: R. D. Irwin, 1980). For another example of this kind of view of strategy, see Benjamin B. Tregoe and John W. Zimmerman, *Top Management Strategy: What It Is and How to Make It Work* (New York: Simon & Schuster, 1980). The authors argue that strategy is "the framework which guides those choices that determine the nature and direction of an organization," implying that strategy involves a pattern of decision making rather than one singular decision.

11. Henry Mintzberg and James A. Waters, "Of Strategies, Deliberate and Emergent," *Strategic Management Journal* 6, no. 3 (July–September 1985): 257–72.

12. For an approach that hews to the emergent strategy model on the foreign policy front, see Maj. Michael Kosuda, "Choosing Grand Strategy," in *The Journal of the United States Military Strategist Association* 1, no. 2 (Fall 2008).

13. J. C. Wylie, *Military Strategy: A General Theory of Power Control*, reprinted with an introduction by John B. Hattendorf (Annapolis, MD: Naval Institute Press, 1989), 14.

14. Charles W. Freeman, *Arts of Power: Statecraft and Diplomacy* (Washington, DC: United States Institute of Peace Press, 1997), 71.

15. Williamson Murray and Mark Grimsley, "Introduction: On Strategy," in *The Making of Strategy: Rulers, States, and War*, eds.Williamson Murray, MacGregor Knox, and Alvin Bernstein (Cambridge, UK: Cambridge University Press, 1994), 1.

16. Andre Beaufre, *An Introduction to Strategy: With particular reference to problems of defense, politics, economics, and diplomacy in the nuclear age*, trans. Maj. Gen. R. H. Barry (Westport, CT: Praeger Publishers, 1965), 22.

17. Luttwak, *Strategy*, ch.1. Edward Luttwak coined the notion of the "logics of strategy," which is related to the assumptions of strategy. He argues that the logics of strategy are often counterintuitive, non-linear, and paradoxical. He argues that strategy, particularly that involving war, involves individuals putting themselves and their organizations voluntarily at high risk, that goes against intuition and human nature. Moreover, part of strategy is making things appear as they are not, something that flies in the face of linearity. So, at the core of strategy is a paradoxical logic.

18. See Abraham Maslow, *Motivation and Personality*, 3rd ed. (New York: Harper, 1954). Maslow's development of the hierarchy of needs gets at the heart of human interests and motivation.

19. Harry R. Yarger, *Strategic Theory for the 21st Century: The Little Book on Big Strategy* (Carlisle Barracks, PA: Strategic Studies Institute, U.S. Army War College, 2006), 5.

20. Beaufre, *An Introduction to Strategy*.

21. See Michael E. Handel's analysis of Clausewitz in *Masters of War: Classical Strategic Thought*, 3rd ed. (Portland, OR: F. Cass, 2001), 104–7.

22. See Jeffrey Record, *A War It Was Always Going to Lose: Why Japan Attacked America in 1941* (Washington, DC: Potomac Books, 2010).

23. Gray, *Modern Strategy*, 361.

24. See Yarger, *Strategy and the National Security Professional*, 18, for an analysis of strategy's holistic logic. Though Yarger doesn't address the question of integration per se, he does argue that strategy requires a fully formed view of the situation.

25. Betts, "Is Strategy an Illusion?," 16. Betts argues that strategy requires predictability and causality. He wrestles with the question of whether oftentimes the connections that are adduced are real or illusory.

26. Yarger, *Strategy*, 16.

27. Betts, "Is Strategy an Illusion?," 16. Also see Hew Strachan, "Strategy and the Limitation of War," ch. 6 in *The Impenetrable Fog of War: Reflections*

on *Modern Warfare and Strategic Surprise*, ed. Patrick Cronin (Westport, CT: Praeger Security International, 2008). Here Strachan emphasizes the theoretical structure provided by strategy in war, and the limitations of this. This is similar to André Beaufre's comment about strategy as original thought.

28. See Richard W. Cottam, *Competitive Interference and Twentieth Century Diplomacy* (Pittsburgh, PA: University of Pittsburgh Press, 1967), ch. 2, for an excellent analysis of the importance of leverage to strategy and the role traditional power factors and strategic interaction play in the creation and use of leverage.

1. SETTING STRATEGIC GOALS

1. See Trita Parsi, "Freeing Israel from its Iran bluff," *Foreign Policy*, May 11, 2011, where he quotes former Mossad chief Meir Dagan as saying that bombing Iran would be a stupid idea, as it wouldn't really achieve its goals and might create other unintended consequences. Also, see Trita Parsi, *A Single Roll of the Dice: Obama's Diplomacy with Iran* (New Haven, CT: Yale University Press, 2012).

2. See Robert J. Art, *A Grand Strategy for America* (Ithaca, NY: Cornell University Press, 2003), 45.

3. This concept of strategic interest was borrowed from Yarger, *Strategy*, 119.

4. Robin Wright and Ellen Knickmeyer, "U.S. Lowers Sights on what can be achieved in Iraq," *Washington Post*, August 14, 2005. Also, see former undersecretary of defense for policy, Douglas J. Feith, *War and Decision: Inside the Pentagon at the Dawn of the War on Terrorism* (New York: Harper, 2008), chs. 6–7, for an insider's explanation of the goals and interests that guided the administration of George W. Bush.

5. See Paul H. Nitze's statement about George Kennan's long telegram that preceded NSC-68 "The Grand Strategy of NSC 68" in James C. Gaston, ed., *Grand Strategy and the Decisionmaking Process* (Washington, DC: National Defense University Press, 1992), 26.

6. John Lewis Gaddis, *Strategies of Containment: A Critical Appraisal of Postwar American National Security* (New York: Oxford University Press, 1982).

7. Yarger, *Strategy*, 136.

8. Deborah Stone, *Policy Paradox: The Art of Political Decision Making* (New York: Norton, 2002), 37–38.

9. Bob Woodward, *Obama's Wars* (New York: Simon & Schuster, 2010), ch. 13.

10. Barack Obama, *National Security Strategy, May 2010*, 25.

11. For a more detailed discussion about the relationship between different levels of goals, and how they relate to different levels within the national security hierarchy, see Luttwak, *Strategy.*

12. See *Bloomberg Business Week*'s interview with Richard Hunter, Dell's head of customer service, "Dell Spiffs Up Its Service," June 12, 2006, http://www.businessweek.com/stories/2006-06-12/dell-spiffs-up-its-service.

13. Catherine Dale, *War in Afghanistan: Strategy, Operations and Issues for Congress* (Washington, DC: Congressional Research Service, March 9, 2011), 8–10.

14. See use of the surge and steady-state terms in the *Quadrennial Defense Review Report* (Washington, D.C., February 6, 2006), 36–40.

15. Barack Obama, *Remarks by the President in Address to the Nation on the Way Forward in Afghanistan and Pakistan* (West Point, NY, December 1, 2009), http://www.whitehouse.gov/the-press-office/remarkspresident-address-nation-way-forward-afghanistan-and-pakistan.

16. See use of the surge and steady-state terms in the *Quadrennial Defense Review Report*, 36–40.

17. Obama, *Remarks by the President.*

18. See Obama, *National Security Strategy*, 23–26.

19. *Quadrennial Defense Review Report.*

2. THE PRIMACY OF CAPABILITY

1. See Thomaz Guedes da Costa, "The Teaching of Strategy: Lykke's Balance, Schelling's Exploitation, and a Community of Practice in Strategic Thinking," ch. 8 in *Teaching Strategy: Challenge and Response*, ed. Gabriel Marcella (Carlisle, PA: Strategic Studies Institute, 2010), 216–19, for an excellent analysis Lykke's discussion of how means (by which he means resources) play into the strategy equation.

2. Betts, "Is Strategy an Illusion?," 6. While not focusing specifically on resources Betts describes strategy as a force multiplier.

3. For a good treatment of the relationship between resources, capability and strategy, see Robert M. Grant "The Resource Based Theory of Competitive Advantage: Implications for Strategy Formulation," *California Management Review* (Spring 1991).

4. MacKubin Thomas Owens, "Strategy and the Strategic Way of Thinking," *Naval War College Review* (Autumn 2007).

5. The 9/11 Commission Report (Washington, DC), 340.

6. Beaufre, *Introduction to Strategy*, 136.

7. R. T. Lenz, "Strategic Capability: A Concept and Framework for Analysis," *The Academy of Management Review* 5, no. 2 (April 1980): 232.

8. *Quadrennial Defense Review Report*, 4.

9. Ibid., 49.

10. Rosabeth Moss Kanter and James Weber, *Gillette Co. (C): Strategies for Change* (Cambridge, MA: Harvard Business School, 2002).

11. Handel, *Masters of War*, 53–63. The notion of a capability linchpin is similar to the Clausewitzian notion of the center of gravity, but it is not identical. For Clausewitz the center of gravity is the hub of all power, which is different but related to the notion of capability.

12. *National Security Strategy, May 2010*, 14.

13. Peter Skarzynski and Rowan Gibson, *Innovation to the Core: A Blueprint for Transforming the Way your Company Innovates* (Boston: Harvard Business School Press, 2008), 18.

14. Joseph Guiltinin, "Launch Strategy, Launch Tactics, and Demand Outcomes," *The Journal of Product Innovation Management* 16, no. 6 (November 1999): 509–29.

3. STRATEGY IN THE DIMENSION OF SYSTEMS

1. Robert Kennedy, "The Elements of Strategic Thinking: A Practical Guide," ch. 2, in Marcella, *Teaching Strategy*, 16.

2. For an excellent treatment of systems analysis for political systems, see Morton A. Kaplan, *System and Process in International Politics* (New York: Wiley, 1957).

3. Charles D. Allen and Glenn K. Cunningham, "Systems Thinking in Campaign Design" in *Guide to National Security Issues*, Bartholomees, 1:3. They argue that a system is a set of units (or elements) that are interconnected in such a way that changes in some elements produce changes in other parts of the system.

4. Michael E. Porter, *Competitive Strategy: Techniques for Analyzing Industries and Competitors* (New York: Free Press, 1980).

5. Fernando F. Suarez, Benjamin Edelman, and Arati Srinivasan, *Symbian, Google & Apple in the Mobile Space* (Cambridge, MA: Harvard Business School, 2009).

6. Hart, *Strategy*, 164. Hart's analysis of indirect vs. direct strategy applies here. Though he doesn't imply a systems strategy, and is much more focused on the enemy, his work on indirect strategy can be applied to our discussion of systems strategies as indirect methods for affecting the

capability and strategic advantage of the opponent. On page 164 he says, "Instead of seeking to upset the enemy's equilibrium by one's attack, it must be upset before a real attack is, or can be successfully launched." This is similar to the analysis that indirect system strategies set the stage by manufacturing leverage, while direct strategies exploit or use that leverage.

7. Handel, *Masters of War*, 33. Sun Tzu's work implicitly deals with system strategies. He argues that prior to direct war, indirect methods should be used like diplomatic and political bargaining, negotiations and deception. He advocates trying to sever the alliances of the enemy, as a precursor to a direct, frontal assault.

8. Ibid., 89. See Clausewitz's analysis of why strategy, though linear in design, becomes non-linear and irrational. He shows how war can careen out of control once launched, and therefore by nature leaves the bounds of rationality.

9. Ibid., 22, gives an excellent comparison between Sun Tzu and Clausewitz. Sun Tzu implies the importance of indirect strategies when he argues that the optimal way of competing is not fighting but convincing the enemy to yield by exhibiting leverage.

10. Hart, *Strategy*, 31. His analysis of Fabian strategies aimed at indirectly draining the capability of an actor that has superior capability, or in my parlance superior situational leverage, is applicable to system strategies.

11. Jan W. Rivkin, *Airborne Express* (Cambridge, MA: Harvard Business School, 2007).

12. Forest L. Reinhardt, Ramon Casadesus-Masanel, and David J. Hanson, *BP and the Consolidation of the Oil Industry, 1998-2002* (Cambridge, MA: Harvard Business School, 2010), 8.

13. Mona Yacoubian, *Syria's Alliance with Iran* (Washington, DC: United States Institute of Peace, May 2007).

14. David E. Bell and Hal Hogan, *7-Eleven, Inc.* (Cambridge, MA: Harvard Business School, 2004). For more on how convenience stores started to emerged in response to the proliferation of large foot-print stores, see the National Association of Convenience Stores (NACS) for information on the history of the growth in the industry.

15. See "International Crisis Group (ICG), Report on Palestinian Strategy, Ramallah, Jerusalem, Washington, Brussels, 26 April 2010 (excerpts)," *Journal of Palestine Studies* 39, no. 4 (Summer 2010): 153.

16. Jim Zanotti and Marjorie Ann Browne, *Palestinian Initiatives for 2011 at the United Nations* (Washington, DC: Congressional Research Service, September 23, 2011).

17. Charles Dhanaraj, Paul W. Beamish, and Nekhil Celly, *Eli Lilly in India: Rethinking the Joint Venture Strategy* (London, Ontario: Richard Ivey School of Business, 2004).

18. Cynthia A. Montgomery and Elizabeth G. Gordon, *Newell Company: Corporate Strategy*, rev. ed. (Cambridge, MA: Harvard Business School, 1999, revised 2005) for a complete analysis of Newell's strategy.

19. Andrew Lee and Michael J. Enright, *Australia's Investment 2000 Proposition* (Hong Kong, China: Center for Asian Business Cases: School of Business, University of Hong Kong, January 1, 2000) for an analysis of Australia's strategy.

20. For an insider view on the assumptions about going into Iraq, see Feith, *War and Decision*.

21. Amy Gurtler, Julie Haimann, Caroline Simmons, "Syrian-Israeli Peace in the Golan: No Walk in the Park," (IMES Capstone Series, The George Washington University, Elliot School of International Affairs, Institute for Middle East Studies, April 2010).

22. Abbas William Samii, "A Stable Structure on Shifting Sands: Assessing the Hizbullah-Iran-Syria Relationship," *Middle East Journal* 62, no. 1 (Winter 2008) for an analysis of the triangular relationship between Iran, Syria, and Hezbollah.

23. See Ross Harrison, "Teaching Strategy in 3D," ch. 10 in Marcella, *Teaching Strategy*. Also, see Jan W. Rivkin and Michael E. Porter, *Matching Dell* (Cambridge, MA: Harvard Business School, 1999).

24. David Arnold, *Procter and Gamble: Always Russia* (Cambridge, MA: Harvard Business School, 1998, revised 2001).

25. W. Chan Kim and Renée Mauborgne, *Blue Ocean Strategy: How to Create Uncontested Market Space and Make the Competition Irrelevant* (Boston, MA: Harvard Business School Press, 2005), for an analysis of how companies can collapse industry boundaries, in effect creating an entire new market.

26. David B. Yoffie and Renee Kim, *Apple Inc. in 2010* (Cambridge, MA: Harvard Business School, 2011) for a synopsis of the company's strategy and historical path.

27. Lt. Col. Larry T. Marek, *The Caspian Sea Pipeline: A Clear Strategic U.S. Interest* (Carlisle Barracks, PA: U.S. Army War College, 2007).

4. STRATEGY IN THE DIMENSION OF OPPONENTS

1. Looking at fencing as an analogue for strategy was developed by Beaufre, *Introduction to Strategy*, 37–41.

2. Suarez, Edelman, and Srinivasan, *Symbian, Google & Apple in the Mobile Space* for how Apple was perceived in 2007 by Symbian, which was the supplier of Nokia's operating system. After the iPhone started to gain market acceptance, Symbian was acquired by Nokia.

3. Gen. Stanley A. McChrystal, "Becoming the Enemy," *Foreign Policy* (March/April 2011): 68.

4. Ray Takeyh, *Guardians of the Revolution: Iran and the World in the Age of the Ayatollahs* (New York: Oxford University Press, 2009), 242–50. He provides an excellent analysis of Iran's nuclear program, from Mohammed Shah to the current Iranian president, Mahmoud Ahmadinejad.

5. Frederic Wehrey et al., *Dangerous But not Omnipotent: Exploring the Reach and Limitations of Iranian Power in the Middle East* (Santa Monica, CA: Rand Corp., 2009), 65.

6. Suarez, Edelman, and Srinivasan, *Symbian, Google & Apple in the Mobile Space*, for how the value chain in the handset industry is structured.

7. Juan Alcacer, Tarun Khanna, Mary Furey, and Rakeen Mabud, *Emerging Nokia?* (Cambridge, MA: Harvard Business School, May 2, 2011), 5, and Juan Alcacer, Tarun Khanna, and Mary Furey, *Nokia: The Burning Platform* (Cambridge, MA: Harvard Business School, May 3, 2011), 1.

8. Amir M. Haji-Yousefi, "Evaluation of Iran's Foreign Policy in Iraq" (Tehran, Iran: Shahid Beheshti University, UNISCI Discussion Papers, January 2006) for a picture of Iran's world view around the time of the U.S. invasion of Iraq.

9. Sun Tzu, *The Art of War*, trans. Ralph D. Sawyer (Boulder, CO: Westview Press, 1994), 77–78, for insights into the importance of attacking the enemy's strategy.

10. Clausewitz, *On War*, 596–97. See his quote about the importance of attacking the opponent's center of gravity, which is the hub of its movement and power.

11. Hart, *Strategy*, 228.

12. Porter, *Competitive Strategy*, for an analysis of how companies compete by differentiating themselves from their competitors.

13. Pankaj Ghemawat and Bret Baird, *Leadership Online (A): Barnes and Noble vs. Amazon.com* (Cambridge, MA: Harvard Business School, May 26, 1998, revised March 16, 2004).

14. Handel, *Masters of War*, 57.

15. Clausewitz, *On War*, 135, 194, 197.

16. Stephen P. Bradley, Pankaj Ghemawat, and Sharon Foley, *Wal-Mart Stores, Inc.* (Cambridge, MA: Harvard Business School, January 20, 1994, revised November 6, 2002), 3, for an analysis of the competitive dynamics between Walmart and K-mart.

17. George Friedman, "Syria, Iran and the Balance of Power in the Middle East," Stratfor Global Intelligence, November 22, 2011.

18. See Christopher M. Blanchard and Jim Zanotti, *Libya: Background and U.S. Relations* (Washington, DC: Congressional Research Service, February 18, 2011) for a good overview of the U.S.-Libya relationship.

19. Beaufre, *Introduction to Strategy*, 24.

20. See Chester A. Crocker's "Reflections on Strategic Surprise," ch. 13 in *The Impenetrable Fog of War: Reflections on Modern Warfare and Strategic Surprise*, ed. Patrick M. Cronin (Westport, CT: Praeger Security International, 2008), for an analysis of strategic surprise. Also, see Sun Tzu, *The Art of War* for his comments on deception and surprise as a force multiplier and an integral part of strategy. Clausewitz, on the other hand, sees deception and surprise as an occasional, but not an integral part of strategy. See Handel, *Masters of War*, 216.

21. Handel, *Masters of War*, 218, for the views of the classical strategists on the use of deception.

22. See Sun Tzu's insights into the importance of attacking the enemy's strategy in Sun Tzu, *The Art of Warfare: The First English Translation Incorporating the Recently Discovered Yin-ch'üeh-shan texts*, trans. Roger T. Ames (New York: Ballantine Books, 1993), 111.

23. Harry G. Summers Jr., *On Strategy: A Critical Analysis of the Vietnam War* (Novato, CA: Presidio Press, 1982), ch. 10.

24. Conversation is recounted by Summers in the introduction to *On Strategy*. According to Summers the conversation took place on April 25, 1975, in Hanoi between Col. Summers Jr., then chief negotiations division, U.S. Delegation, 4 Party Joint Military Team, and Colonel Tu, Chief, North Vietnamese (DRV) Delegation.

25. Hart, *Strategy*, 163.

26. Beaufre, *Introduction to Strategy*, for an analysis of how for every strategic move there is a response from the enemy, which is the basis for the dialectic of opposing, wills.

5. STRATEGY IN THE DIMENSION OF GROUPS

1. Clausewitz, *On War*, VIII: 8, 583, 589–91. Also see the introduction from Summers, *On Strategy* for Clausewitz's musings about the role of the people in the art of war.

2. Cottam, *Competitive Interference*, 228, for an analysis of the role the public plays in the U.S. foreign policymaking process.

3. Scott T. Davis, "Tiring Tehran: A Strategy to Exhaust the Iranian Regime," *The Journal of the United States Military Strategist Association* (Summer

2007). Similar to looking at the opponent's external system, systems analysis can also be used to think about ways to apply pressure on an opponent by shaping its domestic system.

4. Ben D. Mor, "Public Diplomacy in Grand Strategy," *Foreign Policy Analysis* 2, no. 2 (April 2006): 157–76. Also see Joseph S. Nye, *Soft Power: The Means to Success in World Politics* (New York: PublicAffairs, 2004), and by the same author, *The Future of Power* (New York: PublicAffairs, 2011) for an analysis of the role of soft power.

5. See Michael E. Porter and Mark R. Kramer, "Strategy and Society: The Link between Competitive Advantage and Corporate Social Responsibility," *Harvard Business Review* (December 2006).

6. Mor "Public Diplomacy in Grand Strategy," 157–76, for an analysis of how public diplomacy needs to tie into broader strategic initiatives.

7. Jeanne F. Hull, *Iraq: Strategic Reconciliation, Targeting and Key Leader Engagement* (Carlisle, PA: Strategic Studies Institute, September 2009).

8. "Operation IRAQI FREEDOM, January 2007 to December 2008, The Comprehensive Approach: An Iraq Case Study, Executive Summary," (Norfolk, VA: Joint Center for Operational Analysis, February 16, 2010).

9. Marc Lynch, "Explaining the Awakening: Engagement, Publicity and the Transformation of Iraqi Sunni Political Attitudes," *Security Studies* 20, no. 1 (2011): 36–72.

10. Ibid., 46.

11. John A. McCary, "The Anbar Awakening: An Alliance of Incentives," *The Washington Quarterly* 32, no. 1 (January 2009): 49.

12. "Operation IRAQI FREEDOM," 8.

13. Hull, *Iraq*, 14.

14. McCary, "The Anbar Awakening," *The Washington Quarterly* 32, no. 1 (2009): 47.

15. Colin H. Kahl, Michèle A. Flournoy, and Shawn Brimley, *Shaping the Iraq Inheritance* (Washington, DC: Center for a New American Security, June 2008), 18–19.

16. James E. Austin and Cate Reavis, *Starbucks and Conservation International* (Cambridge, MA: Harvard Business School, October 2, 2002, revised May 1, 2004).

17. Ibid., 7.

18. Ibid., 6.

19. Ibid., 8–10.

20. Ibid., 15.

21. Miklos Sarvary and Anita Elberse, *Module Note: Market Segmentation, Target Market Selection, and Positioning* (Cambridge, MA: Harvard

Business School, April 17, 2006), for a quick review of market segmentation concepts.

22. Yarger, *Strategy*, 4.

23. *Dictionary of International Relations Terms* (Washington, DC: Department of State Library, 1987), 85. Also see Charles Wolf and Brian Rosen, *Public Diplomacy: How to Think About and Improve It* (Santa Monica, CA: Rand Corp., 2004).

24. J. Scott Carpenter, Matthew Levitt, Steven Simon, and Juan Zarate, "Fighting the Ideological Battle: The Missing Link in U.S. Strategy to Counter Violent Extremism," A Washington Institute Strategy Report (Washington, DC: The Washington Institute for Near East Policy, 2010) for a piece that shows the importance of the role of public diplomacy strategy in countering terrorism. Also, see Dennis M. Murphy "Strategic Communication: Wielding the Information Element of Power," in *Guide to National Security Issues*, Bartholomees, 1:157–60, for an analysis of strategic communications and public diplomacy.

25. See "U.S. National Strategy for Public Diplomacy and Strategic Communication" *Strategic Communication and Public Diplomacy Policy Coordinating Committee (PCC)*, December 14, 2006, 4, http://www.au.af.mil/au/awc/awcgate/state/natstrat_strat_comm.pdf.

26. Daniel Byman, *The Five Front War: The Better Way to Fight Global Jihad* (Hoboken, NJ: John Wiley & Sons, 2008), 180–85, for an excellent analysis of al-Qaeda's public diplomacy strategy and a viable U.S. response. Also see Col. Timothy J. Loney, "Drafting a New Strategy for Public Diplomacy and Strategic Communication" (Carlisle, PA: U.S. Army War College, 2009).

27. See the notion of the diplomacy of deeds in *U.S. National Strategy for Public Diplomacy and Strategic Communication*, 7. Also, see Mor, "Public Diplomacy in Grand Strategy," 157–76, as an example of thinking that nests public diplomacy within a broader strategic construct.

6. AL-QAEDA'S STRATEGY IN 3D

1. Gladwell, *Tipping Point*.

2. Riedel, *Search for al-Qaeda*, 125 (Kindle Edition).

3. Abu Bakr Naji, *The Management of Savagery: The Most Critical Stage Through Which the Umma Will Pass*, trans. William McCants (Cambridge, MA: John M. Olin Institute for Strategic Studies, Harvard University, 2006) for one of the primary documents uploaded to the internet, presumably by al-Qaeda, in 2004. Also see "The *Al-Qaeda* Manual,"

http://www.fas.org/irp/world/para/manualpart1_1.pdf. The manual was located by the Manchester (England) Metropolitan Police during a search of an al-Qaeda member's home. The manual was found in a computer file described as "the military series" related to the "Declaration of Jihad."

4. Riedel, *Search for al-Qaeda*, 11 (Kindle Edition).

5. Jarret M. Brachman and William F. McCants, *Stealing Al-Qa'ida's Playbook* (West Point, NY: Combating Terrorism Center at West Point, 2006), 7.

6. Riedel, *Search for al-Qaeda*, 32–35.

7. Naji, *Management of Savagery*, 13.

8. Ibid., 21.

9. Riedel, *Search for al-Qaeda*, 33. Also, see also Riedel, "Al-Qaeda Strikes Back" *Foreign Affairs* (May/June 2007): 25.

10. Michael Scheuer, *Through our Enemies' Eyes: Osama bin Laden, Radical Islam, and the Future of America* (Washington, DC: Potomac Books, 2003), 256.

11. Byman, *Five Front War*, 16, for an accounting of the insurgent groups al-Qaeda backed.

12. See MD al-Sulami, "Kingdom worst hit by al-Qaeda Terrorists," *Arab News*, May 3, 2011, which recalls twelve terrorist attacks and seventy random shootings in Saudi Arabia since 2003.

13. Naji, *Management of Savagery*, 17, for a statement about what the Arab satellite states owe the core, the United States.

14. Riedel, *Search for al-Qaeda*, 31–33 (Kindle Edition), for a recounting of these terror attacks on our European allies.

15. Byman, *Five Front War*, 13–32, for an analysis of how al-Qaeda interacts with other regional groups.

16. Brian M. Drinkwine, *The Serpent in Our Garden: Al-Qa'ida and the Long War* by (Carlisle, PA: U.S. Army War College, 2009), 18–19. Also see Naji, *Management of Savagery*, 17, for al-Qaeda's analysis of U.S. capability.

17. Ibid., 20.

18. Riedel, *Search for al-Qaeda*, 7 (Kindle Edition).

19. Naji, *Management of Savagery*, 21–23, for al-Qaeda's comparative view between the Russian and U.S. soldiers.

20. Riedel, *Search for al-Qaeda*, 6.

21. Brachman and McCants, *Stealing al-Qa'ida's Playbook*, 8, on the "vexation and exhaustion" operations of al-Qaeda.

22. Naji, *Management of Savagery*, 14.

23. Byman, *Five Front War*, 16.

24. Carl J. Ciovacco, "The Contours of Al-Qaeda's Media Strategy," *Studies in Conflict and Terrorism* 32, no. 10 (2009): 855.

25. Ibid., 856.

26. Ibid.

27. Christopher M. Blanchard, *Al-Qaeda: Statements and Evolving Ideology* (Washington, DC: Congressional Research Service, July 9, 2007), 6.

28. Ibid.

29. Naji, *Management of Savagery*, 24.

30. Riedel, *Search for al-Qaeda*, 129.

31. Ciovacco, "Contours of al-Qaeda's Media Strategy," 8.

32. Byman, *Five Front War*, 180–82.

33. Jason Burke, "Osama bin Laden Praises Arab Spring in Posthumously Released Tape," *Guardian*, May 19, 2011.

34. Daniel Byman, *Deadly Connections: States that Sponsor Terrorism* (Cambridge, UK: Cambridge University Press, 2005) for an excellent analysis of the role states play in international terrorism.

35. Byman, *Five Front War*, 185–88, for some prescriptive ideas of a negative public diplomacy campaign.

BIBLIOGRAPHY

Art, Robert J. *A Grand Strategy for America*. Ithaca, NY: Cornell University Press, 2003.

Beaufre, Andre. *Introduction to Strategy: With particular reference to problems of defense, politics, economics, and diplomacy in the nuclear age*. Westport, CT: Praeger Publishers, 1965.

Betts, Richard K. "Is Strategy an Illusion?" *International Security* 25, no. 2 (Fall 2000): 5–50.

Binnendijk, Hans, and Richard L. Kugler. *Seeing the Elephant: The U.S. Role in Global Security*. Washington, DC: Potomac Books, 2007.

Bracken, Paul J. *The Second Nuclear Age: Strategy, Danger, and the New Power Politics*. New York: Henry Holt and Company, 2012.

Brzezinski, Zbigniew. *Strategic Vision: America and the Crisis of Global Power*. New York: Basic Books, 2012.

Byman, Daniel, *Deadly Connections: States That Sponsor Terrorism*. Cambridge, UK: Cambridge University Press, 2005.

———. *The Five Front War: The Better Way to Fight Global Jihad*. Hoboken, NJ: John Wiley & Sons, 2008.

Clausewitz, Carl von. *On War*. Translated by Michael Howard and Peter Paret. Princeton, NJ: Princeton University Press, 1976.

Cottam, Richard. *Competitive Interference and Twentieth Century Diplomacy*. Pittsburgh, PA: University of Pittsburgh Press, 1967.

Cronin, Patrick M., ed. *The Impenetrable Fog of War: Reflections on Modern Warfare and Strategic Surprise*. Westport, CT: Praeger Security International, 2008.

Dixit, Avinash K., and Barry J. Nalebuff. *Thinking Strategically: The Competitive Edge in Business, Politics, and Everyday Life*. New York: Norton, 1991.

Drinkwine, Brian M. *The Serpent in our Garden: Al-Qa'ida and the Long War*. Carlisle, PA: U.S. Army War College, 2009.

Freeman, Charles W. *Arts of Power: Statecraft and Diplomacy.* Washington, DC: United States Institute of Peace Press, 1997.

Gaddis, John Lewis, *Strategies of Containment: A Critical Appraisal of Postwar American National Security.* New York: Oxford University Press, 1982.

———. *George F. Kennan: An American Life.* New York: Penguin Press, 2011.

Gladwell, Malcolm, *The Tipping Point: How Little Things Can Make a Big Difference.* New York: Back Bay Books, 2002.

Gray, Colin S. *Modern Strategy.* New York: Oxford University Press, 1999.

Handel, Michael E. *Masters of War: Classical Strategic Thought.* 3rd ed. Portland, OR: F. Cass, 2001.

Hart, B. H. Liddell. *Strategy.* New York: Praeger, 1954.

Kim, W. Chan, and Reneé Mauborgne. *Blue Ocean Strategy: How to Create Uncontested Market Space and Make the Competition Irrelevant.* Boston: Harvard Business School Press, 2005.

Lemay, Benoît. *Erich von Manstein: Hitler's Master Strategist.* Translated by Pierce Heyward. Philadelphia: Casemate, 2010.

Luttwak, Edward N. *Strategy: The Logic of War and Peace.* Cambridge, MA: Belknap Press of Harvard University Press, 1987.

Marcella, Gabriel, ed. *Teaching Strategy: Challenge and Response.* Carlisle, PA: Strategic Studies Institute, U.S. Army College, 2010.

Neustadt, Richard E., and Ernest R. May. *Thinking in Time: The Uses of History for Decision-Makers.* New York: Free Press, 1986.

Nye, Joseph S. *Soft Power: The Means to Success in World Politics.* New York: Public Affairs, 2004.

———. *The Future of Power.* New York: PublicAffairs, 2011.

Ōhmae, Ken'ichi. *The Mind of the Strategist: The Art of Japanese Business.* New York: McGraw-Hill, 1982.

Paret, Peter, ed. *Makers of Modern Strategy: From Machiavelli to the Nuclear Age.* Princeton, NJ: Princeton University Press, 1986.

Porter, Michael. *Competitive Strategy: Techniques for Analyzing Industries and Competitors.* New York: Free Press, 1980.

Rapoport, Anatol. *Fights, Games, and Debates.* Ann Arbor: University of Michigan Press, 1960.

Riedel, Bruce. *The Search for al-Qaeda: Its Leadership, Ideology, and Future.* Washington, DC: Brookings Institution Press, 2008.

Rumelt, Richard P. *Good Strategy Bad Strategy: The Difference and Why It Matters.* New York: Crown Business, 2011.

Stone, Deborah. *Policy Paradox: The Art of Political Decision Making.* New York: Norton, 2002.

Summers, Harry. *On Strategy: A Critical Analysis of the Vietnam War.* Novato, CA: Presidio Press, 1982.

Sun Tzu. *The Art of Warfare: The First English Translation Incorporating the Recently Discovered Yin-ch'üeh-shan texts.* Translated by Roger T. Ames. New York: Ballantine Books, 1993.

Yarger, Harry R. *Strategic Theory for the 21st Century: The Little Book on Big Strategy.* Carlisle, PA: Strategic Studies Institute, U.S. Army War College, 2006.

———. *Strategy and the National Security Professional: Strategic Thinking and Strategy Formulation in the 21st Century.* Westport, CT: Praeger Security International, 2008.

Yip, George S. *Total Global Strategy II: Updated for the Internet and Service Era.* Upper Saddle River, NJ: Prentice Hall, 2003.

INDEX

ABOUT THE AUTHOR

Ross Harrison is a professor in the practice of international affairs in the Walsh School of Foreign Service at Georgetown University. His courses focus on strategy, particularly in the areas of national security, foreign policy, and business strategies. He also teaches Middle East politics in the political science department at the University of Pittsburgh. He is among a group of colleagues (from the U.S. Army War College) that works together to improve the teaching of strategy. With more than thirty years of experience in the area of business strategy, Harrison has been a member of corporate advisory boards and has worked with an international NGO on its strategic challenges.